Hugh Hutton Stannus

A History of the Origin of the Doctrine of the Trinity in the Christian Church

Hugh Hutton Stannus

A History of the Origin of the Doctrine of the Trinity in the Christian Church

ISBN/EAN: 9783337260804

Printed in Europe, USA, Canada, Australia, Japan

Cover: Foto ©Lupo / pixelio.de

More available books at **www.hansebooks.com**

A

HISTORY OF THE ORIGIN

OF THE

DOCTRINE OF THE TRINITY

IN

THE CHRISTIAN CHURCH.

By HUGH H. STANNUS.

WITH AN INTRODUCTION AND APPENDIX
By THE REV. R. SPEARS.

LONDON:
CHRISTIAN LIFE PUBLISHING COMPANY,
281, STRAND,
AND MESSRS. WILLIAMS AND NORGATE, LONDON.

1882.

LONDON
PRINTED BY G. REVEIRS, GRAYSTOKE PLACE, FETTER LANE, E.C.

PREFATORY STATEMENTS.

BIBLE TRUTHS.

" *Hear, O Israel! Jehovah our God is* ONE *Jehovah* ".—
MOSES.

" *The first of all the commandments is, Hear, O Israel, the*
" *Lord our God is one Lord* ".—CHRIST.

" *We know there is none other God but one* ". " *One God*
" *and Father of all who is above all* ". " *One God and one*
" *Mediator between God and men, the man Christ Jesus* ".—
PAUL.

THE TESTIMONY OF EMINENT MEN.

" *For my own part I adhere to the Holy Scripture alone ;*
" *I follow no other heresy or sect. If, therefore, the Father*
" *be the God of Christ, and the same be our God, and if there*
" *be none other God but one, there can be no God besides the*
" *Father* ".—JOHN MILTON.

" *Because it* [*the Trinity*] *is inconsistent with the rule of*
" *prayer directed in the sacred Scriptures. For if God be*
" *three persons how can we pray to Him through His son for*
" *His spirit. . . . For though there be many imaginary*
" *nominal gods, both in heaven and earth, as are indeed all*
" *their many gods and many lords, which are merely*

" *titular; yet to us Christians there is but only* ONE GOD
" THE FATHER, *and Author of all things, to whom alone we*
" *address all our worship and service*".—JOHN LOCKE.

" *There is* ONE GOD, *the Father, ever loving, omnipresent,*
" *omniscient, almighty, the Maker of heaven and earth; and*
" *one Mediator between God and men—the man Christ Jesus.*
" *The Father is the invisible God.* . . . *Christ came not*
" *to diminish the worship of the Father. It is not necessary*
" *to direct our prayers to any other than the Father in the*
" *name of the Son*".—SIR ISAAC NEWTON.

" *Surely I ought to know the God whom I worship—*
" *whether he be a pure and simple being, or whether Thou art*
" *a threefold Deity, consisting of the Father, the Son, and the*
" *Holy Spirit*". . . . " *The Deity is not made up of*
" *three such distinct and separate spirits*".—DR. ISAAC WATTS.

HISTORICAL QUOTATIONS.

" *This doctrine (the Trinity) does not, it appears to me,*
" *belong strictly to the fundamental articles of the Christian*
" *faith; as it appears from the fact that it is explicitly set forth*
" *in no one particular passage of the New Testament.* . . .
" *We find in the New Testament no other fundamental article*
" *besides that of which the Apostle Paul says that other foun-*
" *dation can no man lay than that is laid, the preaching of*
" *Jesus as the Messiah; and the foundation of His religion is*
" *designated by Christ Himself, the faith in the only true God*
" *and in Jesus Christ whom he hath sent*".—NEANDER.

" *While for so many centuries, of all the Christian doc-*
" *trines, that of a Trinity in Unity has been considered the*
" *most obscure and mysterious, in the writings of the apostles*

v

" *there is no trace of any scruple which it created. It seems*
" *to have called for no explanation, and it is not even spoken of*
" *as a mystery*".—BISHOP HIND.

" *The whole Christian system was still* [2nd century] *com-*
" *prised in a few precepts and propositions; nor did the*
" *teachers publicly advance any doctrines besides those contained*
" *in what is called the Apostles' Creed.*" . . . " *The*
" *Council of Constantinople, assembled by Theodosius the Great*
" [*in the fourth century,* 381] *gave the finishing touch to*
" *what the Council of Nice had left imperfect, and fixed in a*
" *full and determinate manner the doctrine of three persons in*
" *one God*".—MOSHEIM.

" *In the fifth century Christianity had conquered Paganism*
" *and Paganism had infected Christianity. The Church was*
" *now victorious and corrupt. The rites of the Pantheon had*
" *passed into her worship, the subtleties of the Academy into*
" *her creed. In an evil day, though with great pomp and*
" *solemnity—we quote the language of Bacon—was the ill-*
" *starred alliance stricken between the old philosophy and the*
" *new faith. Questions widely different from those which had*
" *employed the ingenuity of Pyrrho and Carneades, but just*
" *as subtle, just as interminable, and just as unprofitable,*
" *exercised the minds of the lively and voluble Greeks. When*
" *learning began to revive in the West, similar trifles occupied*
" *the sharp and vigorous intellects of the schoolmen. There*
" *was another sowing of the wind and another reaping of the*
" *whirlwind*".—MACAULAY.

" *Before I shall conclude this head, it is requisite I should*
" *inform thee, reader, concerning the origin of the Trinitarian*
" *doctrine:—Thou mayest assure thyself, it is not from the*
" *Scriptures nor reason, since so expressly repugnant; although*
" *all broachers of their own inventions strongly endeavour to*

" *reconcile them with that holy record. Know then, my*
" *friend, it was born above three hundred years after the*
" *ancient Gospel was declared; it was conceived in ignorance,*
" *brought forth and maintained by cruelty; for though he that*
" *was strongest imposed his opinion, persecuting the contrary,*
" *yet the scale turning on the Trinitarian side, it has there con-*
" *tinued through all the Romish generations.*"—WILLIAM
PENN.

" *The true reformed religion (or, if you please, the truly old*
" *religion) is the Holy Scriptures (or the sum of the faith in*
" *them, the Apostles' Creed) and holy life. . . . . . In*
" *the appendages and circumstantials of Christianity, in fine,*
" *scholastic, improved notions, charity, peace, and meekness*
" *become us,—not zeal. . . . . Give me leave to demand*
" *of the world a reason why Christian communion should not*
" *be left at that latitude at which Christ and his apostles in*
" *Holy Scripture have left it? To this, if men would addict*
" *themselves (and why should they not) all schisms would*
" *soon be at an end*".—BISHOP WETENHALL.

CONTENTS AND ARGUMENT.

THE strict and absolute unity of God is a first principle of the Bible. The entire scope and spirit of both the Old and New Testament are distinctly on the side of the *uni-personality* of God. The Jews, who made Monotheism their boast and glory, never charge Christ, or the first teachers of Christianity, with originating any new theory of the Godhead. Christ and the apostles spoke of the Father as the "ONLY " TRUE GOD". It is repeatedly admitted by Trinitarians that the word " *Trinity* " is not in the Bible; and that in the earliest records of our religion, not only the word Trinity is not to be found, but no equivalent of the word, nor any proposition that intimates God is three persons. An additional fact, confirmatory of the sole Deity of God the Father, is found in Christ's instruction and example of prayer, which were followed during the first two centuries. The two or three texts in the Bible supposed by some to *foreshadow*, or *hint* at, or *imply* the Trinity, receive at the hands of Trinitarian scholars a very simple and rational explanation, which lends no countenance to the theory of a plurality of persons in the Godhead. The doctrine of the Primitive Church is found in the Scripture, and also in the Apostles' Creed; the doctrine of later times in the Nicene and Athanasian Creeds. The word Trinity, familiar to schools of philosophy, was introduced into Christian literature about the close of the second century. The Pagan Trinities of the Egyptian, Assyrian, and Hindoo systems of religion (and also of Platonic philosophy) were popular at the time of the first planting of Christianity. The origin and developement of the doctrine of a Triune Deity in the Church is clearly traced to Platonic and other influences during the third and fourth centuries. Its introduction caused considerable discussion, agitation, and strife during the period named. The Council of Nice (A.D. 325) voted in favour of the Deity of Christ; the Council of Constantinople (A.D. 381) fixed the doctrine of the Trinity. From that time the Roman Emperors resolved and proclaimed they would punish all Christians who would not believe in and worship three persons in one God. The following chronological data may aid the reader of this treatise to mark the progress of the doctrine, from the close of the second to the close of the fourth century:—

A.D.

1.—Monotheism the boast and glory of the Jews.

29.—About this time Jesus said, "The first commandment is, the Lord " our God is one Lord" * * * * "The true worshippers shall " worship the Father".

32.—About this time Jesus said, "I ascend unto your Father and my "Father, your God and my God".

57.—About this time Paul wrote, "There is none other God but "one". . . . "To us there is but ONE God the Father and "one Lord Jesus Christ".

96.—About this time Clement wrote, "Christ was sent by God and "the Apostles were sent by Christ".

120.—The Apostles' Creed begins to be known to the Church. It says, "I believe in God the Father Almighty".

150.—Justin Martyr about this time began with Platonic teaching to corrupt Christian simplicity.

170.—The word *Trias* first occurs in Christian literature.

200.—The word *Trinitas* is first used by Tertullian.

230.—Origen writes against prayers being offered to Christ.

260.—Sabellius teaches,—Father, Son, and Holy Spirit, are three names for the same God.

300.—No Trinitarian forms of prayer are yet known to the Church.

310.—Lactantius (orthodox father) writes, "Christ never calls himself "God".

320.—Eusebius writes, "Christ teaches us to call his Father the true "God, and to worship Him".

325.—The Nicene Council agree to call Christ, "God of God, very "God of very God".

350.—Great conflicts in the Church about the doctrine of the Trinity.

370.—The Doxology, "Glory to the Father, to the Son, and to the Holy "Ghost", composed, and complained of as a novelty.

381.—The Council of Constantinople gives the finishing touch to the doctrine of "three persons in one God".

383.—The Emperor Theodosius threatens to punish all who will not believe in and worship the Trinity.

From this date Arianism rapidly declines. In A.D. 451, the doctrine of the two natures of Christ becomes an established dogma. "Glory "be to the Father, and to the Son, and to the Holy Ghost", is ordered to be sung in all Churches, A.D. 529. The Clergy are commanded, A.D. 669, to commit to memory the Athanasian Creed. Bishop Basil required the Clergy, A.D. 826, to repeat this Creed every Sunday.

INTRODUCTION.

CONSIDERATIONS, BIBLICAL AND HISTORICAL, WHICH SUPPORT THE DOCTRINE OF THE ABSOLUTE ONENESS OF GOD.

THERE is an increasing belief that the creeds, generally accepted among the Churches, differ very widely from the statements of the Sacred Volume, and from the doctrines which were common in the first period of the Christian Church. On no question is this more striking than on that which refers to the Unity of God. While there is not the slightest hint in the Old Testament or the New of a plurality of persons in the Godhead, the doctrine of a Triune deity is spoken of at the present time, and has been for ages, as a fundamental doctrine of the Christian faith.

All Christians are persuaded that God has revealed himself to us in the Holy Scriptures ; and all agree that there is ONE GOD and Father of all, and that this doctrine is certified by revelation, and accords with enlightened reason. Yet a very grave divergence appears on the question of the absolute Unity of God. There are those who, when speaking of God, are satisfied with the simple and magnificent language of the Bible, that "there is one God ; and there is "none other but He"; while there are others who speak of the Godhead as a Trinity composed of Father, Son, and

Holy Ghost. With respect to this difference which has divided Christians, "what saith the Scripture"?

In making our appeal to the Sacred Volume, we may be allowed to recall to the memory of our readers the memorable words of Chillingworth:—"The Bible, I say, "the Bible only is the Religion of Protestants. Whatsoever "else they believe besides it and the plain, irrefragable, "indubitable consequences of it, well may they hold it as a "matter of opinion; but as a matter of faith and religion, "neither can they with coherence to their own grounds "believe it themselves, nor require the belief of it of others. ". . . . He that believes the Scripture sincerely, and "endeavours to believe it in the true sense, cannot possibly "be an heretic".

THE TESTIMONY OF THE BIBLE TO THE UNITY OF GOD.

"Holy Scripture containeth all things necessary to salvation".— *Articles of the Church of England.*

On a question of such vital importance to the simplicity of belief and the purity of worship, as the UNITY of God, we go to the Bible. We learn in the clear, precise, and unequivocal language of its pages, that there is "ONE God "and there is none *other"*; and this statement being in perfect accord with every chapter and verse of both Old and New Testament, we may fairly speak of it as a first principle of divine revelation. There are not only thousands of texts which teach this, but the entire complexion of the Bible sets forth the sole deity of ONE PERSON, called the God of Abraham, Isaac, and Jacob, and also repeatedly said to be "the God "and Father of our Lord Jesus Christ".

In the following and other texts God is styled "ONE":— "Jehovah our God is *one* Jehovah"—Deut. vi. 4. "In that

" day there shall be *one* Jehovah, and his name *one*"—Zech.
" xiv. 9. "Have we not all *one* Father? Hath not *one* God created
" us"—Malach. ii. 10. " For *one* is your Father who is in
" heaven"—Matt. xxiii. 9. "There is none good but *one*,
" that is God"—Mark x. 18. "The Lord our God is *one*
" Lord"—Mark xii. 29. "There is *one* God, and there is
" none other"—Mark xii. 32. "Seeing it is *one* God who
" shall justify"—Rom. iii. 30. "There is none other God
" but *one*"—I. Cor. viii. 4. "To us there is but *one* God
" the Father"—I. Cor. viii. 6. " *One* God and Father of
" all"—Eph. iv. 6. "Thou believest there is *one* God; thou
" doest well"—James ii. 19.

It appears to us impossible for language to be more
plain, precise, and emphatic as to the doctrine that God is
one Being, *one* Person, *one* Mind, than the statements in the
texts we have quoted. We may ask what words, what
possible combination of words or sentences, could make
more clear the strict unity of the *One* supreme, "the King
" eternal, immortal, invisible, the *only* wise God". If the
divine Being is not one person, but three persons in one
God—if this is really a fundamental doctrine of the
Christian religion,—we ask for a single sentence from any
part of the Bible which says so. Dr. South admits, " It
" must be allowed that there is no such proposition as this,
" 'that one and the same God is three different persons',
" to be found formally and in terms in the Sacred Writings".[1]

There are other classes of texts confirmatory of this
doctrine, the Unity of God. We are all aware of the
emphatic and pronounced way in which the singular pronoun

---

[1] Considerations on the Trinity, p. 38.
Professor Hey, of Cambridge (Lectures II. 25), says, "The term
" *Trinity* not being Scriptural, we cannot adhere to Scripture and yet
" use that."

and verb are used of the divine Being:—"*I* am the
" Almighty God", Gen. xvii. 1 ; "*I* am that *I* am ", Exodus
iii. 14 ; "Do not *I* fill heaven and earth ", Jer. xxiii. 24.

Every page in the Bible abounds with this evidence
in such forms of speech as "*thine* O Lord is the greatness ",
"*thine* is the Kingdom ", &c., bearing repeated witness to
the ever-repeated truth of both reason and revelation, that
" Jehovah our God is ONE ".

There are, however, two or three texts in the Old
Testament where the plural is found in relation to God :
—"Let *us* make man in our image"; "The man is
" become as one of *us*". John Calvin says of the text,
"The man is become as one of us": "From this place
" many Christians infer the doctrine of three persons in the
" Godhead ; but I fear the argument is not valid". And
Dr. Croft, a learned Trinitarian, says :—"Perhaps too much
" stress is laid upon the expression, ' Let *us* make man in our
" ' image.' The plural is frequently applied to one only ;
" and the language of consultation is evidently used in con-
" descension to human infirmity ".[2] In addition to these
texts with the plural pronoun, it is only fair to add that
in most places of the Hebrew scriptures the word translated
God is *Elohim.* This is the plural form ; *El* and *Eloah*
being the singular. On this the late Dr. Campbell, of Aber-
deen, says, " that Luther stood up for the Trinity from the
" word Elohim, but Calvin refutes his argument, or quibble
" rather, at some length".[3] Professor Stuart admits the
weakness of this argument in the following words :—"For
" the sake of emphasis, the Hebrews commonly employed
" most of the words which signify Lord, God, &c., in the

---

[2] Sermon in 1786 in the Bampton Lectures. Similarly Dr. South,
Grotius, Mercer, Limborch, Rosenmuller, and others.

[3] Lectures on Systematic Theology, p. 489.

" plural form, but with the sense of the singular".[4] We could
easily fill pages with the concessions of scholarly Trinitarians
on these two points, that neither the word Elohim nor the
few plural pronouns are to be regarded as evidence of a
plurality of persons in the Godhead.

Continuing the Scripture proof, there are numerous
passages in which our heavenly Father is styled the
"Holy One", the "Mighty One", the "High and Lofty
" One", &c. "I am Jehovah, the Holy One, the Creator of
" Israel, your King"—Isa. xliii. 15. "I have not concealed
" the words of the Holy One"—Job vi. 10. "Unto thee will
" I sing with the harp, O thou Holy One of Israel"—Ps.
lxxi. 22. " For thus saith the High and Lofty One that inha-
" biteth eternity"—Isa. lvii. 15. "Therefore thus saith the
" Lord Jehovah of Hosts, the Mighty One"—Isa. i. 24, &c.
&c. Here we would remark that, while we find texts speaking
of God as the Holy One, the Mighty One, &c., in the singular
number, there is an entire absence from the Bible of phrases
such as the Holy Three, the Mighty Three, and the like.
This could not have been the case had the doctrine of
"three Persons in one God" been revealed or known to the
authors of the Sacred Volume. In view of these things
Bishop Beveridge may well say that, "the Jews, though
" they had the law three thousand years, and the pro-
" phets above two thousand years, yet to this day
" they never could make this [the Trinity] an article of
" Faith".[5] It seems almost incredible that any intelli-

---

[4] Grammar of Hebrew Language, p. 180. Similarly Michaelis,
Buxtorf, and others. We refer our readers to twelve pages of such
admissions in "Wilson's Concessions of Trinitarians", to which we are
much indebted. If the argument from ELOHIM proved anything, it
would prove, as in the ascription in Hebrews, chap i. 9, to Christ, "thy
" throne O ELOHIM," that a plurality of divine persons existed in Christ.

[5] Private Thoughts, part ii. p. 66. Similarly Bishop Tostat, Bishop
Blomfield, Archbishop Lawrence, and others.

gent person, who has carefully read the Bible, can claim it
as a support of the doctrine of a Trinity of Persons in
the Godhead. The authors of the Sacred Volume appear
to have been totally unacquainted with such a view of the
nature of God.

It may be said that "the term *God* includes the person of
"Jesus Christ and also the Holy Ghost". This is an
assumption not only without proof, but opposed to repeated
statements of Christ himself, as well as of the sacred writers,
who constantly speak of God as the "God and Father of Jesus
"Christ". On the cross Christ said, "My God, my God, why
"hast thou forsaken me"—Matt. xxvii. 46. And afterwards
he said, "I ascend unto my Father and your Father, unto my
"God and your God"—John xx. 17. He spoke of God as
being distinct from himself as one person is from another. "I
"came from God"—John viii. 42. "Why callest thou me
"good? there is none good but one, that is God"—Mark
x. 18.

It is difficult, if not impossible, to suppose that the disciples
as they walked and talked with our Saviour, thought they were
holding converse with the Almighty God Himself. The
late Archbishop Longley admits this:—"I should therefore
"be prepared to expect that the grand disclosure of Christ's
"divine nature would not be formally made to them till that
"period .   .   .   the descent of the Holy Ghost".[6] They

---

[6] The Brothers Controversy, p. 54—57. Cardinal Newman (in his
"Arians of the Fourth Century", p. 55—a book written when he was
a clergyman of the Established Church), says, "The most accurate
"consideration of the subject will lead us to acquiesce in the statement as
"a general truth, that the doctrines in question [viz., the Trinity and
"Incarnation] have never been learned merely from Scripture". Dr.
Bennet ("Discourse of the Trinity", ch. viii. p. 94), says, "During the
"time of our Saviour's ministry, the disciples did not believe he was any-
"thing more than a mere man, conducted and assisted by the Spirit of

thought and spoke of Christ both before and after the day
of Pentecost as "a man approved of God"—Acts ii. 22.
He "increased in wisdom and stature, and in favour with
"God and man"—Luke ii. 52; "He prayed to God"—
Luke vi. 12; "He had come from God and went to God"
—John xiii. 3; "God made him Lord and Christ"—
Acts ii. 36; "the Head of Christ is God"—1 Cor. xi.
3; "He is at the right hand of God" — Acts ii. 33:
"God raised him from the dead"—Acts ii. 32; "God
"has given him a name above every name"—Phil. ii. 9:
and, finally, "He shall deliver up the kingdom to God, even
"the Father . . . then shall the Son also himself be
"subject unto Him that put all things under him, that God
"may be all in all"—1 Cor. xv. 28. Every student of the
New Testament knows that such passages as the above
abound in its pages. Evidence like this demonstrates
that Christ is a person as distinct from God as the
disciples were distinct from Christ, or from one another.
A writer who carefully examined the New Testament
says "that 1326 times the word *God* is applied to a person
"distinct from Jesus Christ". With a clearness and a force
of language that cannot be surpassed, Christ, the brightest
example of a religious life and a religious teacher, has
taught that God is his God and Father, as He is our God
and Father.[7] Why need we doubt his word, or hold a theory
of him, or of our heavenly Father, out of accord with all he
taught? Perplexing, indeed, and constantly perplexing,

"God", and "There is not in all the New Testament one passage which
"implies that the disciples during his ministry believed him to have any
"divine nature". Bp. Burgess ("Plain Argument for the Divinity of
"Christ", § 6) admits, "The apostles appear not to have known that
"Christ was God till after his resurrection and ascension".

[7] John xx. 17.

must all the preceding texts be to those who hold that " there are three persons of equal power and glory in the " Godhead ".

When we are told that there are two other persons of equal power and glory to God the Father (and He, the Father of Christ, was the only God known to the Jews), we are reminded of texts like the following :—" There is none like " me"—Exod. ix. 14 ; " For who in the heaven can be " compared unto Jehovah "?—Ps. lxxxix. 6 ; " For who is " like unto Jehovah our God"?—Ps. cxiii. 5 ; " To whom " then will ye liken God ? . . . or shall I be equal ? saith " the Holy One"—Isa. xl. 18-25 ; " There is none like unto "Thee, Jehovah . . . none like unto Thee "—Jer. x. 6, 7 ; " Who is a God like unto Thee "?—Micah vii. 18. We need not quote further evidence that the God-inspired prophets had no idea of any other person or persons of equal power and glory to their Jehovah God. Also the whole tenor of the worship of the first apostles is as adverse to the Trinitarian theory as is anything in the Old Testament.

Yes, strictly corroborative of the views of patriarchs, prophets, and psalmist, as to the absolute Unity of God, is the teaching of Jesus Christ and his apostles ; and they still further strengthen this doctrine by their instruction and example about prayer and worship.[8] Christ prayed to the Father, and taught his followers that " the " true worshippers shall worship the Father", "for the " Father seeketh such to worship Him "—John iv. 23. He

---

[8] Abp. Wake (in his work on the Catechism, p. 130) says that the Lord's Prayer teaches us " that we should pray to God only, and to " Him as our Father through Jesus Christ our Lord ". Jeremy Taylor (Works xiii. 143) says, " That the Holy Ghost is God is nowhere said " in Scripture. That the Holy Ghost is to be invocated is nowhere com- " manded ; nor any example of its being done, recorded ".

says, " In that day ye shall ask *me* nothing "—John xvi. 23.
There is no command or exhortation in the New Testament
to worship any being other than " the God and Father of
" our Lord Jesus Christ ". Paul says, " I worship the God
" of my fathers "—Acts xxiv. 14. " I bow my knees unto
" the Father of our Lord Jesus Christ "—Eph. iii. 14. This
is the uniform language of the New Testament. Precept and
example are plentifully found for this, and only this. Christ
in his prayer addresses God as " the only true God "—
John xvii. 3. It is not until hundreds of years after
apostolic times that we find in the Christian Church a
prayer to "the holy, blessed, and glorious Trinity, three
" persons and one God". Christ himself, after his ascension,
was never addressed by any of his disciples, except
on occasions when, as to Stephen and to Paul, he was
actually and visibly appearing to them.

In view of the importance of the Scriptural argument
for the strict UNITY of God, we do not ask those who
hold a different opinion from ourselves to produce many
texts of Scripture which contain a clear statement of their
doctrine of the Trinity ; we ask for *one* text only. We are told
by scholarly Trinitarians that there is no such text. Luther
rightly says :—" The word *Trinity* is never found in the Divine
" Records".[9] Hooker says more than this :—" Our belief in
" the Trinity, the co-eternity of the Son of God with his
" Father, the proceeding of the Spirit from the Father and
" the Son, these with such other principal points are in Scrip-
" ture nowhere to be found by express literal mention ; only
" deduced they are out of Scripture by collection ".[10]
Pages could be filled with similar testimony from the works of

---

[9] Postil Major, fol. 282 ; Confut. Rat. Latom, tom. ii. fol. 240.

[10] Eccles. Polity, book i. § 14.

scholarly Trinitarians. They virtually concede that it is a doctrine of inference and of church authority. And let it be remembered, this is done notwithstanding the express statements of the sacred volume; such as the following:—"Hear O " Israel, Jehovah our God is one Jehovah ". " I, even I, am " HE, and there is no God with ME". "Thou shalt have none " other God but ME ". " In that day there shall be *One* " Jehovah, and his name ONE". " Jesus answered, the first " of all the commandments is, Hear O Israel ! the Lord our " God is ONE Lord ". " This is life eternal that they " might know THEE, THE ONLY TRUE GOD, and Jesus Christ " whom thou hast sent ". " There is ONE God, the Father". " God is one". " When ye pray, say, Our Father". "The " true worshippers shall worship the Father".

It has been said, and we endorse the statement, that so far as facts and arguments go, the question between the two theologies, the Trinitarian and the Unitarian, is as completely settled as the question between the two astronomies : the old, which makes our earth the centre around which sun, moon, and stars revolve every twenty-four hours ; and the new, which makes our earth a lesser planet in our solar system, which is but one among countless systems of worlds. With the facts fairly presented and considered, it is no more possible to believe in the old theology than in the old astronomy. And all that we have to do is to set the facts fairly before the people.

CONCESSIONS OF TRINITARIANS.

" There is this distinction which attaches to us, that the sense which " we put upon important passages is the *very sense* given to them by " Orthodox writers ".—*Madge.*

An array of texts, such as we have presented, may appear like special pleading or an *ex parte* statement on the side of the absolute unity of God; for it is sometimes said that the advocates of every different theory or church system can find texts in the Bible for their views. To this we are able to reply, that learned defenders of the doctrine of the Trinity acknowledge the deficiency of Scriptural evidence for their views. Bishop Smalridge says truly, " It must be owned "that the doctrine of the Trinity, as it is proposed in our " Articles, our Liturgy, our Creeds, is not in so many words " taught us in the Holy Scriptures. What we profess in " our prayers we nowhere read in Scripture, ' that the one " ' God, the one Lord, is in person not one only, but three "' persons in one substance.' There is no such text in " Scripture as this, that ' the Unity in Trinity, and the "' Trinity in Unity, is to be worshipped '. No one of the " inspired writers hath expressly affirmed that in the Trinity " none is afore or after other, none is greater or less than " another."[1] And Neander, in his Church History,[2] says, " This doctrine [the Trinity] does not, it appears to me, belong " strictly to the fundamental articles of the Christian Faith; " as appears from the fact that it is explicitly set forth in no " particular passage of the New Testament; for the only " one in which this is done, the passage relating to the " three that bear record (1 John v. 7), is undoubtedly " spurious, and by its ungenuine shape testifies to the fact " how foreign such a collocation is from the style of the " New Testament writings. We find in the New Testament " no other fundamental article, besides that of which " the Apostle says, that other foundation can no man " lay than that is laid—the preaching of Jesus as the " Messiah; and the foundation of his religion is designated " by Christ himself as the faith in ' the only true God, and

---

[1] Sixty Sermons ; Sermon. xxxiii. p. 348.

[2] History of the Church, Bohn's Edition, Vol. II. p. 286.

"'in Jesus Christ whom he hath sent'". Luther, as we have seen, admits "The word Trinity is never found in the "Divine Records, but is only of human invention. Far "better would it be to say *God* than *Trinity*".[3] Calvin says:—"I dislike this vulgar prayer, 'Holy Trinity, one "'God, have mercy on us', as altogether savouring of "barbarism".[4] Dr. South goes further than Luther and Calvin, and says:—"It must be allowed that there is no "such proposition as this, that *one and the same God is* "*three different persons*, formally and in terms to be found "in the Sacred Writings, either of the Old or New Testa-"ment; neither is it pretended that there is any word of the "same significance or importance with the word *Trinity*. "used in Scripture with relation to God".[5] It would be easy to multiply concessions such as the following:— "We ought to believe that there are three persons in one "essence in the Deity, God the Father, God the Son, and "God the Holy Ghost, though you never find in Scripture "these sublime and remarkable words".[6] So that when Cardinal

---

[3] "*Trias* is first found in the writings of Theophilus. *Trinitas*, in "the writings of Tertullian".—Schaff. "If Theophilus was the first "who employed the word *Triad*, *Trinity*, that abstract term, which was "already familiar in the schools of philosophy, must have been intro-"duced into the theology of the Christians after the middle of the "second century".—Gibbon's Roman History, vol. iii., chap. 21.

[4] Tractat. Theol., p. 796.

[5] Consid. on the Trinity, p. 38.

[6] Cochlæus. Bishop Beveridge gives (" Tracts for the Times", vol. iii., p. 30, No. 77) the doctrines "that three distinct Persons are to be "worshipped—Father, Son, and Holy Ghost—and that each of these "is very God . . . . . ; and that Christ is very God and very "man in one and the same person ", as instances of doctrines which are not read expressly and definitely in Holy Scripture. "This I call "at once dogma [the Trinity] and above our comprehension. If they "be intelligent agents, they must have three independent wills of their

Wiseman asked the question, " Where is the term Trinity to " be discovered in Scripture "?[7] he asked a question which is capable of only one answer, not as a matter of opinion but as a matter of fact, that not only the term *Trinity*, but no statement or definition of the doctrine, is to be found in the Bible. The Rev. James Carlile says:—"I have ever disliked " the use of the word *Trinity* in prayer to God, as not being a " name whereby God reveals Himself to us, and as " savouring of scholastic theology ".[8] We would once more remind our readers that the above are all concessions of Trinitarian divines, who most justly observe that *none* of the terms used in speaking of the Trinity are to be found in the Sacred Volume.

When we are told that texts may be produced from the Bible to uphold any theory, we can meet the assertion by the simple truth, that there is *no* text in the Bible in which there occurs the phrase "Trinity", or "Three persons in one God", or " Father, Son, and Holy Ghost are one God", or any other equivalent of the doctrine taught in the creeds of the churches. This important fact is conceded by many scholarly divines who profess the Trinitarian faith. In a very recent work, a Rural Dean, the Rev. T. Mozley, brother-in-law to Cardinal Newman, writes as follows:—"I ask with all humble " ness where the idea of Threeness is expressed in the New " Testament with a doctrinal sense and force ? Where is the " Triune God held up to be worshipped, loved, and obeyed ? " Where is He preached and proclaimed in that threefold

" own, and what becomes then of the Unity of the Deity ? . . . . " We cannot be called upon to believe that which we do not understand, " and which, after all, is only handed down to us by tradition ".—*The late Duke of Sussex.*

[7] Lectures on Doctrines, &c., p. 270.

[8] Jesus Christ the Great God, p. 232.

" character? We read 'God is one', as too, 'I and the Father
" 'are one'; but nowhere do we read that Three are one,
" unless it be in a text long since known to be interpolated.
" . . . . To me the whole matter is most painful and
" perplexing, and I should not even speak as I now do, did
" I not feel on the threshold of the grave, soon to appear
" before the Throne of all truth. . . . Certainly not in
" Scripture do we find the expression 'God the Son', or
" 'God the Holy Ghost'. Whenever I pronounce the name
" of God, simply and first, I mean God the Father, and I
" cannot help meaning that, if I am meaning anything".[9]

THE TESTIMONY OF HISTORY.

" Christianity conquered Paganism, but Paganism infected Chris-
" tianity. The rites of the Pantheon were introduced into her institu-
" tions, and the subtleties of the Academy into her creed."[1]—*Macaulay.*

If there be one fact in the history of the Christian religion
more striking and demonstrable than another, it is this, that
our religion started its career with a purely Monotheistic
theology. We have already shown that there is not a single
sign in the pages of the Gospels, or of the Acts of the
Apostles (the first records of our religion) of any attempt
to introduce any different theological conception of the
Unity of God than that which for ages had been known to the
Jewish people.[2] It would appear that the Christian religion

[9] Reminiscences of Oriel College and the Oxford Movement.

[1] Essay on Lord Bacon.

[2] " The systematic doctrine of the Trinity was kept in the back-
" ground in the infancy of Christianity, when faith and obedience were
" vigorous".—Dr. J. H. Newman's "Arians of Fourth Century",
11 i., p. 160.

is not singular in the changes which have taken place since its first promulgation. Writers on such religions as those of the ancient Egyptians, the Brahmins, and others, contend that a much greater theological simplicity marked their earlier than their later career.[3]

No historian ignores the serious conflicts which took place during the third and fourth centuries in the Christian Church. Mosheim says that "it is certain that human "learning and philosophy have at all times pretended "to modify the doctrines of Christianity, and that these "pretensions have extended further than belongs to the "province of philosophy on the one hand, or is consistent "with the purity of the Gospel on the other".[4] The Platonic philosophy, Gibbon says, "anticipated one of the "most surprising discoveries [the Trinity] of the Christian "revelation".[5] Bishop Horsley concedes that "Platonic "converts to Christianity applied the principles of their old "philosophy to the explication and confirmation of the "articles of their faith. They defended it by arguments

---

[3] " It is apparent to me that the Christian religion has been corrupted " from very early times, and that these corruptions have been mistaken " for essential parts of it, and have been the cause of rendering the " whole religion incredible ".—*The Duke of Grafton.*

[4] History of the Christian Church: Second Century.—" The Hellenic " philosophy operated from without, as a stimulating force, upon the " form of the whole patristic theology, the doctrines of the Logos and " the Trinity among the rest ".—Schaff's History of Christian Church, vol. i., p. 284. " Those who maintained that learning and philosophy " were rather advantageous than detrimental to the cause of religion, " gained by degrees the ascendant ".—Mosheim, Second Century, Part 2. As there are numerous editions of Mosheim's work, and various translations, we quote passages as under the century in which they are to be found. Our quotations are from Maclaine's translation, 1810.

History of the Roman Empire, vol. iii., chap. 21.

" drawn from Platonic principles, and even propounded it in
" Platonic language ".[6]   Mosheim says of the first three centuries, " Nothing was dictated to the faith of Christians in the
" matter [of the Trinity]; nor were any modes of expression
" prescribed or requisite to be used in speaking of this
" mystery ".[7]   Similarly, the late Bishop Hind remarks, " It
" seems to have called for no explanation, and is not even
" spoken of as a mystery".[8]   "These doctrines", says Dr.
Olinthus Gregory, " concerning the nature of the Trinity,
" which in preceding ages had escaped the vain curiosity of
" man and had been left undefined by words and undetermined
" by any particular set of ideas, excited considerable contests
" through the whole of this [fourth] century".   Surely a
doctrine of which it is so repeatedly said, by *Trinitarian
historians*, that " we find no trace of any words " which set
it forth during the first centuries ; that "there was no mode
" of expression prescribed in speaking of it "; that " it was
" left undetermined and undefined by any set of ideas";
that it " called for no explanation" ; that it "was kept in the
" background"; "that it was not even spoken of as a
" mystery "—could not have had much influence in that

----

[6] Collected Charges, p. 130; London 1830.   A school of Platonists at Alexandria (see " Cudworth's Intellectual System ") taught,
that in the Godhead were (1) The supreme good: (2) the mind or
intellect: (3) the soul.   And that the *second* was generated from the
first, and the *third* was dependent on the first and second.   All Church
historians affirm, with Bishop Horsley, that the Platonic doctrines were
forced on the attention of the early Christians.   Athanasius, Bishop of
Alexandria, used to tell the Arians to go and learn the Trinity from the
Platonists.   St. Augustine confesses that he was in the dark about the
Trinity until he read some Platonic writings " which the providence of
" God had thrown in his way."

[7] History of the Christian Church.

[8] History, Rise, &c., of Christianity, p. 35.

primitive, heroic, and martyr age of the Church, even if it then had any existence among Christians.

It is generally admitted that the three creeds, the Apostles', the Nicene, and the Athanasian, mark successive stages of development in the doctrine of the Trinity. Mosheim says of the first two centuries of Christianity, " The Christian system as it was hitherto taught, preserved " its native and beautiful simplicity, and was comprehended " in a small number of articles. The public teachers incul-" cated *no other doctrines* than those taught in the Apostles' " Creed". . . . Everything beyond the reach of com-" mon capacities was carefully avoided ".[9]

It was the Council of Nice, A.D. 325, which introduced the Nicene Creed. But it was the Council of Constantinople, A.D. 381, that gave the finishing touch to the doctrine which the Council of Nice had left imperfect of THREE PERSONS IN ONE GOD, and that branded with infamy all errors and set a mark of execration upon all heresies.[10]

From this time the arm of the State came forth to sustain what the subtleties of philosophy had introduced into the Christian Church. Here is a decree[11]—21st Feb., A.D. 380— of which no one can mistake the meaning :—" We, the " three Emperors, *will* that all our subjects follow the " religion taught by St. Peter to the Romans, professed

---

[9] History of the Christian Church (Second Century, Part II.).

[10] The words of Mosheim are (Fourth Century, Part II.) " A " hundred and fifty Bishops who were present at this Council [Con-" stantinople, A.D. 381] gave the finishing touch to what the Council of " Nice had left imperfect, and fixed in a full and determinate manner " the doctrine of three persons in one God . . . they branded with " infamy all the errors, and set a mark of execration on all the " heresies ".

[11] Codex Theodos, xvi., 1, 2. See " Milman's History of Christianity ", vol. i., chap. 9.

" by those saintly prelates, Damasus, Pontiff of Rome, and
" Peter, Bishop of Alexandria, that they believe the one
" divinity of the Father, Son, and Holy Spirit, of majesty
" co-equal in the Holy Trinity. We *will* that those who
" embrace this creed be called Catholic Christians. We
" brand all the senseless followers of other religions by the
" infamous name of heretics, and forbid their conventicles
" to assume the name of Churches.   We reserve their
" punishment to the vengeance of Heaven, and to such
" measures as divine inspiration shall dictate *to us*".   This
decree appeared in the names of Gratian, Valentinian II., and
Theodosius.   It was the official notification of the doctrine
of the Trinity ; and thus, as Dean Milman puts it in his
" History of Christianity", "the religion of the whole Roman
' world was enacted by two feeble boys and a rude Spanish
" soldier ".[12]   Waddington, a Trinitarian, says that only
two years after the Council of Constantinople, " Theodosius
" addressed the Arians, A.D. 383, thus, 'I will not permit
" 'throughout my dominions any other religion than that
" 'which obliges us to worship the Son of God, in unity of
" 'essence with the Father and the Holy Ghost, in the
" 'adorable Trinity'. . . . As Theodosius persevered
" inflexibly against the Arians, and his severities were
" attended by general and lasting success, the doctrine of
" Arius, if not perfectly extirpated, withered from that
" moment rapidly and irrecoverably ".[13]   The testimony of
Gibbon is very similar: " In the space of fifteen years
" Theodosius issued no less than fifteen severe edicts, more
" especially against those who rejected the doctrine of the
" Trinity ; and to deprive them of every hope of escape, he

[12] History of the Christian Church (A.D. 383), chap. 9.

[13] History of the Christian Church (A.D. 383), chap. 7.

"sternly enacted that if any laws or rescripts should be
"alleged in their favour, the judges should consider them as
"the illegal productions of either fraud or forgery".[14]

It is clear, that toward the close of the fourth century, the
Church had arrived at a period when a new nomenclature
had been successfully introduced into its creeds and prayers.
The simple and Scriptural Monotheism of the Jews, and of the
first Christian Church, was completely gone.[15] The doctrine
of the Trinity, the offspring of heathen mysticism, philosophy and sophistry, was set up. This change did not
come without serious conflicts, protests, and convulsions.
The whole of the fourth century bears witness to this.
Men of learning espoused different sides in this theological warfare. The mass of the people raised the
voice against the innovation. Epiphanius writes, A.D.
350, that the short, plain argument of the body of
the people in his time was, "Well, friend, what doctrine
"now? Shall we acknowledge *one* God or *three* Gods"?[16] Other
disputes quickly sprung up on nice points. One of these

---

[14] History of Roman Empire, vol. iii., chap. 27.

[15] "In the article of the Trinity, the Christian conception of God
"completely defines itself in distinction alike from the abstract Mono-
"theism of the Jewish religion, and from the polytheism and dualism
"of the heathen".—"Schaff's History of the Christian Church," vol. i.,
p. 282.

[16] See Priestley's "History of the Corruption of Christianity", and
also "Early Opinions", for other similar statements. "For nothing is
"more manifest than this truth, that the noble simplicity and dignity of
"religion were sadly corrupted in many places when the philosophers
"blended their opinions with its pure doctrines". . . . . "The
"sacred and venerable simplicity of the primitive times, which required
"no more than a true faith in the Word of God, and a sincere obedience
"to His holy laws, appeared little better than rusticity and ignorance
"to the subtle doctrines of this quibbling age".—*Mosheim, under the
Fourth Century.*

was on the question whether we ought to say "One of
"the Trinity suffered in the flesh", or "One person of the
"Trinity suffered in the flesh".   On this pretty puzzle there
were many different opinions.   From that day to this the
doctrine of the Trinity has been the subject of differences so
constant and serious that we are inclined to think Christendom will soon say, what Archbishop Tillotson once said of
the Athanasian Creed, "I wish we were well rid of it".[17]

In concluding this part of our task, we cheerfully
acknowledge the fact that, on the question of the Unity of
God, men of equal intelligence and devotion are found on
different sides.   The names of illustrious divines, scholars,
and others, who for fifteen hundred years have graced the
Church and the world with their learning and goodness,
and who at the same time believed in the doctrine of
the Trinity, are well known.   But it is also true that in
the earlier period of the Church,[18] as in modern times, not

---

[17] Letter to Bishop Burnet.   The Council of Ephesus (431) decreed
that Mary was "the mother of God".   After this a dispute arose on
the question of Anne, the mother of Mary, whether she should be
called, "the mother of the mother of God", or, "the grandmother of
"God".   One absurdity paves the way for another.

[18] We claim not only the first apostles and teachers of Christianity,
but the great body of the "noble army of martyrs and confessors", of
the ante-Nicene period, as having held the strict unity of God.   The
ante-Nicene fathers invariably spoke of Christ as subordinate to the
Father.   In the third and fourth centuries there was a Trinity held up
to be believed in, but not a Trinity of equal persons in the Godhead.
"All the learned men in the second century agree in saying that the
"Christians worship only one God, the God of Abraham, Isaac, and
"Jacob".—*Bouzique.*   The following are words of Origen, "We must
"pray only to God, the Father of all, to whom the Saviour prayed.
".   .   .   .   In this we are all agreed, and are not divided about the
"method of prayer".   The prayer of Polycarp, when he was tied to
the stake, shows very clearly to whom prayer was then addressed: "O
"Lord God Almighty, the Father of thy well-beloved and blessed Son
"Jesus Christ, by whom we have received a knowledge of Thee", &c.

a few whose names are household words in Christendom for virtue and learning have held the Scriptural and Unitarian view of God. JOHN MILTON was a careful and industrious student of the Bible. Yet the following are words of his, in a treatise he wrote against the Trinity:—" For " my own part, I adhere to the Holy Scriptures alone, I " follow no other heresy or sect. If, therefore, the Father " be the God of Christ, and the same be our God, and if " there be none other God but one, there can be no God " beside the Father ".

Sir Isaac Newton, it is well known, was a devout reader of the Bible. Yet all acquainted with his theological opinions admit that he adopted Unitarian views. He says :— " There is One God, the Father, ever living, omnipresent " omniscient, almighty, the maker of heaven and earth, and " one mediator between God and men—the man Christ " Jesus. The Father is the invisible God, whom no eye " hath seen or can see. All other beings are sometimes " visible. All the worship (whether of praise, or prayer, or " thanksgiving) which was due to the Father before the " coming of Christ, is still due to him. Christ came not to " diminish the worship of his Father ".

With Milton and Newton there is another name constantly associated, as sharing the same distinguished mental rank, JOHN LOCKE. The evidence of his Unitarian belief is so complete that no one now denies that he held the same theological opinions on this subject as the poet and the philosopher.[19] He had well considered the Scriptural, and also the historical, arguments for and against the Trinity. He says, "The fathers before the Council of Nice speak " rather like Arians than the orthodox." . . . "There " is scarcely one text alleged by the Trinitarians which is not

---

[9] See Lord Chancellor King's " Life of Locke ".

" otherwise expounded by their own writers." . . .
" It [the Trinity] is inconsistent with the rule of prayer
" directed in the Sacred Scriptures.   For if God be three
" persons, how can we pray to Him through His Son for
" His Spirit"?

Towards the close of a long and active life, the celebrated
Dr. ISAAC WATTS was constrained to abandon his former
Trinitarian views.   We have the clearest evidence of this in his
" Solemn Address to the Deity ", in which occurs the following :—" Dear and blessed God, hadst Thou told me plainly
" in any single text that the Father, Son, and Holy Spirit are
" three real, distinct persons in Thy divine nature, . . .
" I should have joyfully employed all my reasoning powers,
" with their utmost skill and activity, to have found out this
" inference, and engrafted it into my soul. . . . The
" Deity is not made up of three such distinct and separate
" spirits".

With the names of Milton, Locke, Newton, and Watts, we
can associate those of Chillingworth, Lord Falkland, Sir M.
Hale, Dr. Samuel Clarke, Whiston, Whitby, Benson, Lardner,
Porson, William Penn, Sir W. Jones, Hales of Eton, and others,
who made the Bible and theology a speciality of their studies.
Poets like Akenside, Barbauld, Rogers, Joanna Baillie, Roscoe,
Bryant, Longfellow, Emerson; and philosophers like Priest-
ley, Franklin, Hutcheson, Price, Rittenhouse, Cavendish, and
De Morgan, also embraced this simple faith in ONE GOD, the
Father.   It was adopted in the last century by five eminent
Bishops of the Established Church, Rundle, Clayton, Watson,
Law (of Carlisle), and Law (of Elphin).[20]   Brewster says that
" England may well be proud of having had Milton, Locke,
" and Newton for the champions of Protestantism ";—and we
can also say that our views of the absolute unity of God

[20] Others add, Bishop Hoadley.

have been honoured by the testimony of these and other learned men. Still we place our reliance, for religious truth, on the Word of God, not on the wisdom of man. To the law and the testimony we appeal—to the Bible, and the Bible only, as the religion of Protestants.

Bible Texts Supposed to Refer to the Trinity.

" There is scarcely one text alleged by the Trinitarians which is not otherwise expounded by their own writers ".[1]—*John Locke.*

In quoting the language of eminent Trinitarian divines who say that " the word Trinity is never found in the " Divine Records ", that " you never find in the Sacred Scrip- " tures 'three persons in one God' "—that " the phrase Holy " Trinity is dangerous and improper "—that " there is no " such proposition as that one and the same God is three " persons "—" where in the Scriptures is the Triune God " held up to be worshipped, loved, and obeyed "?—we do not wish to convey the idea that our Trinitarian neighbours do not produce any texts from the Bible as indirect support of their views. We know they do advance Scriptural proofs ; but the fewness of such texts is notable. In Wesley's " Sermon on the Trinity", one text alone, 1 John v. 7, is relied on. This is now removed from the New Testament as spurious. In the "Complete Analysis of the Bible," by the Rev. Nath. West, D.D., a most extensive work, four texts are relied on; one of these, as we have already said, is removed. In this work there are probably five hundred texts on the person of Christ, and only four texts as Scriptural proofs of the Trinity. In Dr. Eadie's "Classified Texts of the Bible ", a most elaborate work, like Dr. West's, founded on 'Talbot's "Analysis of the Bible", while there are twenty-eight

[1] Common Place Book.

pages of texts devoted to the person of Jesus Christ, there
are only six texts adduced as Bible proofs of the Trinity.
Let us examine these, and we shall find that what John
Locke said of the concessions of Trinitarians is verified.

(1) Isa. xlviii. 16 : "The Lord God and His spirit hath
"sent", &c. We have before us over a dozen concessions on
this text, but let the words of Luther and Calvin suffice.
Luther says, "This passage has been amazingly darkened.
"The Jews understood it of the prophet; and this opinion I
"adopt. . . . It will not validly support the mystery of
"the Trinity". Calvin says, "Many apply it to Christ, but
"they are not supported by the language of the prophet.
"We should beware of violent and forced interpretations".*

(2) Matt. iii. 16, 17 : "The spirit of God descending like
"a dove, and lighting upon him; and lo a voice from heaven,
"saying, 'This is my beloved son, in whom I am well pleased'".
There is nothing said here of three co-equal and co-eternal
persons in the Godhead. We agree with the words of a
Calvinistic commentator on this text, that "the spirit of God
"is said to come upon men when they are eminently quali-
"fied to undertake any great office"—*Rosenmüller.* "The
"epithet beloved, given to the Son on this occasion, marks
"the Father's greatness of affection for him"—*Macknight.*
"This is my Son whom I have sent on purpose to reveal my
"will by him; and whatsoever he teaches comes from me,
"and is perfectly my will or law"—*Hammond.* When Dr.
Adam Clarke says, "This passage affords no mean proof of
"the doctrine of the Trinity", we reply there is no proof
here of three persons in the Godhead. All Christian Unitarians, as well as Trinitarians, believe in Father, Son, and

---

* "Eminent theologians, as Jerome, Vatablus, Calvin, our own Dutch
divines, and others, will have these to be the words of Isaiah to himself".
—Witsius on the Creed, Diss. vii. 15.

Holy Spirit. It would be a great mistake to infer from this that all believe that these three are one God.

(3) Matt. xxviii. 19, "Go ye, therefore, and teach all "nations, baptising them in the name of the Father, and of "the Son, and of the Holy Spirit". On this text Michaelis remarks, "We know how frequently this passage is quoted "as a proof of the doctrine of the Trinity. . . . I must "confess I cannot see it in this point of view. The eternal "Divinity of the Son which is so clearly taught in other "passages is not here once mentioned, and it is impossible to "understand from this passage, whether the Holy Ghost is a "person. The meaning of Jesus may have been this : Those "who were baptised should, upon their baptism, confess "that they believed in the Father, and in the Son, and in "all doctrines inculcated by the Holy Spirit ".[3] We are at one with the view of this divine, and also with Rosenmüller, who says, "We are baptised into the Father, "as the Author of a new religion ; into the Son, as the "Lord of a new Church ; and into the Holy Spirit, as "the guardian and assistant of this Church ". We have before us other testimonies, such as "Though the three persons "are indeed named, no mention is made of a unity of "essence and of a real distinction of persons ".—*Nihusius.*

(4) 2 Cor. xiii. 14 : "The grace of the Lord Jesus Christ, "and the love of God, and the communion of the Holy "Ghost". In this passage, as in all others which mention the Father, Son, and Holy Ghost, nothing is said of their being one God. We all believe in the Father as the only true God. We believe in the Son as the messenger of God; and in the Holy Spirit as a gift from God. We use most freely the New Testament language touching the Father, Son, and Holy Spirit, while we hold that there is not the least sugges-

---

[3] The Burial, &c., of Jesus Christ, pp. 325—327.

tion in it of a tri-personal Deity. "These and the like words ",
says Hammond, "are a form of greeting which includes in
" it all good wishes, but not a solemn prayer to those persons
" named in the form".

(5) It must be noted as a very remarkable thing that the
only passage in which Father, Word, and Holy Spirit are
spoken of as One (1 John v. 7) is excluded from the Revised New Testament as spurious.

(6) Another text quoted by Dr. Eadie is, "For through
" him we both have access by one spirit unto the Father".
It must puzzle the most ingenious person to discover how
this proves that there are three persons in the Godhead.

We will now quote, without comment, certain other texts
which we have known produced as Scriptural evidence
of the Trinity, which show how hard pressed the defenders of the doctrine must have been to have had
recourse to them:—Ps. xxxiii. 6, "By the word of Jehovah
" were the heavens made, and all the hosts of them by the
"breath of his mouth".   Numb. vi. 24, "Jehovah bless thee
"and keep thee: Jehovah make his face to shine upon thee:
"Jehovah lift up his countenance upon thee".   Isa. vi. 3,
"And one cried unto another and said, Holy, holy, holy is
"Jehovah of hosts".   Isa. xxxiv. 16, "Seek ye out of the
"book of Jehovah and read: . . .   his mouth it hath
"commanded, and his spirit it hath gathered them".
1 Cor. xii. 4-6, "There are diversities of gifts but the
"same spirit, and there are diversities of administration
"but the same Lord ; and there are diversities of operations
"but it is the same God who worketh all in all".   Rev. i. 4-5,
"Grace be unto you and peace from Him who is, and who
"was, and who is to come, and from the seven spirits that
"are before the throne, and from Jesus Christ".   On these
texts learned Trinitarians have wisely said that the *triple*

use here and there of words like "Jehovah," or the word "Holy" is a very unsubstantial proof of so important a doctrine. Grotius remarks, "Surely such repetitions are " void of mystery ; and imply nothing but the unparalleled " excellence of the thing spoken of, or some extraordinary " emotions of the speaker".[4] Calvin says, "Plainer texts " ought to be adduced, lest in proving the chief article of " our faith we should become the ridicule of heretics". But where are those plainer texts? We are not aware of any texts, except the above, which have been used as Bible proofs of the Trinity. Again we challenge anyone to find us *one* passage in the whole compass of the Bible where the doctrine of three persons in one God is stated or even hinted at. It is only "by inference" says one, "by collection " says another, " by the authority of the Church," says another, that we derive the doctrine of the Trinity.

The first teachers of Christianity were never charged by the Jews (who unquestionably believed in the strict unity of God), with introducing any new theory of the Godhead.[5] Many foolish and false charges were made against Christ ; but *this* was never alleged against him or any of his disciples. When this doctrine of three persons in one God was introduced into the Church, by new converts to Christianity, it caused immense excitement for many years.[6] Referring to this, Mosheim writes, under the fourth century, "The subject of "this fatal controversy, which kindled such deplorable divisions "throughout the Christian world, was the doctrine of Three

---

[4] "The threefold repetition is thought to have so little of an argument in it as to scarcely merit any answer".—*Dr. South.*

[5] "Monotheism was the proud boast of the Jew ".—Canon Farrar, " Early Days of Christianity", vol. i., p. 55.

[6] " In the Fourth Century", says Jortin, vol. ii., p. 60, " were held " thirteen Councils against Arius, fifteen for him, and seventeen for the " semi-Arians,—in all, forty-five ".

"Persons in the Godhead; a doctrine which in the three "preceding centuries had happily escaped the vain curiosity "of human researches, and had been left undefined and "undetermined by any particular set of ideas".

Would there not have been some similar commotion among the Jewish people in the time of Christ, if such a view of the Godhead had been offered to their notice, and if they had been told that without belief in this they " would perish everlastingly " ?

Concluding Chapter.

" When we say God hath revealed anything, we must be ready to " prove it, or else we say nothing. . . . Some men seem to think " that they oblige God by believing plain contradictions, but the matter " is quite otherwise".—*Archbishop Tillotson.*

While there is no mention in the sacred Scriptures of a Trinity of persons in the Godhead, it is equally certain that in the field of nature no hints or suggestions of it are to be seen. "Where is the people to be found", asks Robert Hall, "who learned the doctrine of the Trinity " from the works of nature "?[1] It is true that by the light of nature many of our race have been led to believe in the existence and the providence of God; but the mystery of the Trinity has in no instance been shadowed forth in the glory of the heavens, in the beauty of the earth, or in any of the forms or combinations of matter. Many divines who have had an interest in finding all the support they can for this view of God, declare, like Dr. John Owen, that " Nature " recoils from the doctrine";[2] or, like Hackspan, that "From

1 Works, vol. v., pp. 534-5.

² Divine Origin of the Scriptures, p. 132.

"' the principles of nature the Trinity cannot be made known to us ".[3]

It is not only admitted by learned Trinitarians that there is no mention of a Triune Deity in the Bible, and no suggestion of that doctrine in the phenomena of nature, but, in addition, it is stated that this view of the Godhead is hostile to reason. Cardinal Wiseman asks, " Who will pretend to say that he can, by any stretch " of his imagination, or of his reason, see it possible how " three persons in one God can be but one Godhead"?[4] Dr. Hey, a Cambridge Divinity Professor, also confirms this statement in the following passage :—"When it " is proposed to me to affirm, that in the unity of " the Godhead there be three persons, ... I " profess and proclaim my confusion in the most unequivocal " manner".[5] Dr. South has pronounced the result which this doctrine involves, " so very strange and unaccountable, that " were it not adored as a mystery it would be exploded as a " contradiction ".[6] " That three Beings should be one " Being," says Soame Jenyns, "is a proposition which " certainly contradicts reason—that is, *our* reason ".[7] The language of Bishop Beveridge sets the matter in the clearest light, as an inconceivable mystery : "That God the Father " should be one perfect God of himself, God the Son one " perfect God of himself, and God the Holy Ghost one " perfect God of himself; and yet that these three should " be one perfect God of himself, so that one should be

[3] Notes, &c., tom. i., p. 534.

[4] Lectures on Doctrines of the Church, p. 370.

[5] Lectures in Divinity, vol. ii., pp. 249, 251, 253.

[6] Sermons, vol. iii., p. 240.

[7] A View of the Internal Evidence of Christian Religion, p. 140 (sixth edition).

" perfectly three and three perfectly one ; that the Father,.
" Son, and Holy Ghost should be three and yet be one, but
" one and yet three !   O heart-amazing, thought-devouring,
" unconceivable mystery !"[8]   In view of this doctrine, and
its relation to the scheme of redemption, Bishop Hurd
confesses that at it " reason stands aghast, and faith herself
" is half confounded " ![9]

Now, if it be true that the Christian religion is a simple,
natural, and rational religion, and if it be impossible so to
describe the doctrine of " three persons in one God ",
the question may well arise, whether this doctrine forms.
any part of the Christian system.   The strict and
absolute unity of God is the doctrine of the Bible, and
accords with the works of nature and the intelligence and.
reason of man.   All the forms of prayer which we find
in the Bible are invariably addressed to *one* God,
one Mind, *one* Person.   There are no appeals in the
sacred volume to a " holy, blessed, and glorious Trinity,.
" three persons in one God "; the idea of God is every-
where strictly Monotheistic.   This truth of the UNITY of
God appears clear, and the proofs of it are as abundant as
blades of grass on the landscape, or as leaves in the forest.
The language of the Bible, about God, endorses the plain language of nature, reason, and common sense.   Why, then, do so
many of our brethren fall back on inconceivable mysteries and
palpable contradictions?   Why does the great body of the
Christian Church suffer itself to be trammelled by the jargon
of a scholastic theology, and by notions about our heavenly
Father which have completely obscured the " simplicity of
" Christ ", and introduced creeds and forms of worship not

---

[8] Private Thoughts on Religion, art. iii., pp. 52-3.

[9] Sermons at Lincoln's-inn, vol. ii., No. xvii.

only unknown to the pages of the New Testament, but opposed to both its letter and spirit.

While the source of the doctrine of a tri-personal God is not to be found in the Bible, it can be traced to pagan notions and scholastic subtleties, which the writer of the following pages—the Prize Essay—has laid open. We are not without hope that the intelligence of the present age, aided by the wide diffusion of the Scriptures, will speedily lead the great body of thinking Christians to the re-discovery of (what Sir Isaac Newton once called) "that long-lost truth of the Gospel, the Unity "of God". The philosopher is not alone in his wish for Church reform. Neander, the historian and theologian, gives utterance to a similar hope in the words of Wickliffe. " I look forward to the time when some brethren, whom " God shall condescend to teach, will be thoroughly con- " verted to the primitive religion of Christ, and that such " persons, after they have gained their liberty from Anti- " Christ, will return freely to the original doctrines of Jesus;. " and then they will edify the Church, as did Paul ".

As the year 1881 was the fifteen-hundredth anniversary of the authoritative promulgation of the doctrine of the Trinity, a prize of fifty guineas was offered for the best Essay on the " Origin of the Doctrine of the Trinity in the Christian Church." Some thirty fairly well-written Essays were sent to the editor of THE CHRISTIAN LIFE *newspaper, who had offered the prize. To Hugh Hutton Stannus, Esq., of London, the writer of the following Essay, the prize was awarded. The judges unanimously agreed that no prize could be given for an Essay received on " The Injurious Effect of the Doctrine of the Trinity upon the Simplicity, Power, and Success of Christianity."*

ROBERT SPEARS.

22, Gascoyne-road, Victoria Park, London.
December, 1882.

THE ORIGIN AND DEVELOPEMENT

OF THE

DOCTRINE OF THE TRINITY

IN THE CHRISTIAN CHURCH.

------◆------

§ 1. The DOCTRINE—held by Patriarchs, taught by Prophets, and preached by Jesus Christ our Saviour, and his Disciples—THERE IS ONLY ONE GOD, THE FATHER—has been shown to be the only and exclusive theology of the Bible. It is, nevertheless, a fact that contrary opinions have been, and are still, held by many earnest and pious souls; and have been dominant in the Christian Church for a considerable length of time. The arguments from the *Numerousness* of believers and the *Antiquity* of the belief must be fairly met by those who seek to bring back the Christian religion to its original purity.

§ 2. The Bible doctrine—of the undivided Unity of God —will, with any candid inquirer acknowledging the appeal to the Scriptures, be sufficient to dispose of the argument from Majorities ; and the object of this short Essay is to deal with the argument from Antiquity, and present a brief digest showing to such as have not leisure to study the Ecclesiastical Histories, how various and differing doctrines of the Trinity were gradually developed, and added to the original Unitarian form of Christianity preached by the Saviour and recorded in the Gospels.

D

§ 3. Historic Theology ascertains not only facts, but also their contributory causes ; and thus enables us to trace Developement. By its help we can show the approximate dates of the various accretions, from the times of the Apostles until they were authoritatively adopted, and a "finishing touch" put to the doctrine of the Trinity at the Council of Constantinople, just fifteen centuries ago, A.D. 381.

§ 4. The writer trusts not to offend the sentiments of any fellow-Christian, feeling bound to extend to those who differ the same consideration he would claim for himself. He knows well that the whole superstructure of the doctrine in question had its origin in one of the highest and holiest of human motives—the grateful desire to do honour to that Saviour who has done so much for us—and he thinks its holders should be tenderly dealt with, even though they, by this doctrine, lessen the Glory of God.

§ 5. The subject will be treated in two broad divisions:—

(*a*) The belief in Trinities by various Pagan peoples before the time of Jesus—*e.g.* the Egyptians, Assyrians, Hindoos, &c.; and

(*b*) The introduction and gradual developement of a Trinity inside the Christian Church.

For the sake of brevity,* only those opinions which have had an important influence in this developement will be mentioned.

§ 6. Trinities are the product of the second, or combining stage of Mythologies. They are more subtle than the simple deities formed by the personification of natural phenomena or human passions. They may have been *Partnerships* of

---

* The Essay was limited to "about 5000 words."

separate individuals, or unions of different *Attributes* in one individual.*

I.—PAGAN TRINITIES.

Egypt.

§ 7. The Egyptian priests indulged in much metaphysical speculation, holding that everything perfect must have three parts. Thus they divided the being of man into three :—

(*a*) The animal,

(*b*) The intellectual, and

(*c*) The spiritual;

and each of these again into three modes of action; and each mode of action into three relations. They divided their God Horus into three parts or persons :—

(*a*) Horus the King,

(*b*) Horus-Ra, and

(*c*) Horus the Scarabæus;

And other of their Gods in similar manner.

---

* It was formerly claimed by its upholders that the doctrine of the Trinity was *the* peculiarly Christian doctrine; but this statement is now admitted to be erroneous, and its defenders are constrained to concede the existence of Trinities amid the superstitions of pre-Christian Paganism. Some explain the fact by suggesting that the ideas had been " imparted to the descendants of Noah and the Patriarchs, and " have reached the Egyptians through that channel, and have been " preserved and embodied in their religious system." It is called an " important secret ;" and the *complete silence* of the Old Testament on this doctrine is said to have resulted from " wise caution " (!) (Sir J. G. Wilkinson, " Manners and Customs of the Ancient Egyptians," Second Series, vol. i., pp. 186-8). Canon Trevor, in his interesting little work on " Ancient Egypt," published by the Religious Tract Society, also speaks of these " triads," and regards them as relics of the first hope and expectation of fallen man, *i.e.* the promised seed (p. 139). If the " wise caution " system of Biblical exegesis be permitted, there are few superstitions which could not be foisted into Christianity. To what shifts are the defenders of this venerable corruption reduced ! [See also the Note to § 23.]

§ 8. They also combined various attributes to make Trinities. Thus the Sphinx is composed of :—

(*a*) Man, typifying Intelligence,

(*b*) Ox, typifying Fruitfulness, and

(*c*) Lion, typifying strength.

The well-known architrave ornament also consists of :—

(*a*) The Globe, typifying the Creative power,

(*b*) The Wings, typifying the Preserving power, and

(*c*) The Serpent, typifying the Destroying power.

Their Gods were similarly treated, each city having its own Trinity made up of its favourite Gods. Thus —

At Thebes:	Amun-Ra,
	Maut, and
	Chonso.
At Aboo-Simbel:	Phthah,
	Amun-Ra, and
	At-hor.
At Philæ :	Osiris,
	Isis, and
	Horus.

Sir J. G. Wilkinson, p. 185, says :—" In these triads the " third member proceeded from the other two ; that is, from " the first and second. . . . . The third member of a triad, " as might be supposed, was not of equal rank with the " two from whom it proceeded." It might be suggested that these were *Partnerships ;* but here we have a " triad " described in the same work, vol. i. pp. 231 *et seq.*, consisting of—

(*a*) Bait,

(*b*) At-hor, and

(*c*) Akori ;

and it is addressed, " Hail trimorphous God:" ΧΑΙΡΕ ΤΡΙΜΟΡΦΕ ΟΕΟΣ (*sic* in orig., prob. ΘΕΟΣ).

§ 9. Other instances might be given, but the above will be sufficient ; and their importance in the developement will be seen when the Alexandrine [Egyptian] philosophy of the centuries preceding Christ is mentioned.

India.

§ 10. In the earlier Hindu mythology, that of the Vedas, about 1000 B.C., the chief Gods were :—

(*a*) Agni, *i.e.* Fire, presiding over the Earth,

(*b*) Indra, *i.e.* the Firmament, presiding over the Mid-air, and

(*c*) Surya, *i.e.* the Sun, presiding over the Heavens ;

and these three are asserted over and over again to be forms of one God. (1)   This is Nature-worship, growing out of their agricultural pursuits.   There were then no professional priests: each man performed the religious ceremonies for his own household.

§ 11. Gradually, in the course of centuries, a sect of priests grew up, and superstition became rampant ; until at length in the later or Puranic times they claimed to be the only mediators between the people and the Gods.   The word for Prayer is "brahm," and a Prayer-bearer [or priest] is a "brahman."   The simple service of prayer and praise became invested with a sacrificial or propitiatory character ; and the priests argued that if prayer could move the Gods it must be greater than they, and gradually the idea of Prayer became personified, till Brahma became the chief God in the Hindu Pantheon.   The "Trimurti", or Trinity, was then:—

(*a*) Brahma, as the Creative power,

(*b*) Vishnu, as the Preserving power, and

(*c*) Siva, as the Transforming power.

Although at first these were only *powers*, yet round each soon gathered accretions of personal relations and genealogies; as happens in all anthropomorphic* theologies.

§ 12. The existence of these Trinities did not prevent the invention of countless other deities; † in fact, when once the great simple statement "Jehovah is one Jehovah"‡ is passed, there is no limit to the multiplication of lesser objects; as may be seen in the worship paid to Saints and Images in India.

§ 13. The Buddhists are not Trinitarians, but they teach the *possession* by Buddha of the bodies of men, which with other mystical doctrines was brought from India after the expedition of Alexander, B.C. 325; and thus they contributed towards the Developement.

Assyria.

§ 14. In the palace erected at Khorsabâd by Sargon,** B.C. 720, were the well-known Bulls. These are Trinities:—

(*a*) The Human head, typifying Wisdom,

(*b*) The Bull's body, typifying Power, and

(*c*) The Eagle's wings, representing Omnipresence.

This is a Trinity of Attributes similar to the Egyptian ones in § 8. There were also combinations of Fours in their sacred symbolism; and the prophet Ezekiel in his first

---

* *i.e.* theologies which describe their gods as having the *shapes of men*.

† Thus "Varuna is the chief of a group of deities which are only a "*splitting-up* and in some sort the reflection of his own being" (Barth, "The Religions of India", Trübner, 1882, p. 19).

‡ Deut. vi. 4, quoted by Jesus, Mark xii. 29.

** Called Shalmaneser in 2 Kings xviii.

vision* probably employed them to convey his meaning, as being types well known to his fellow captives.†

II.—PHILOSOPHIC THEORIES.

Platonism.

§ 15. Plato, B.C. 360, a Greek of Athens, was the con-necting link between the mystic philosophy of the Egyptians, and that of his successor, Philo. After studying under Socrates, in Greece, he travelled to Egypt, where he became imbued with the oriental practice of allegorising which is apparent in his speculations.

§ 16. His first doctrine [probably derived from Socrates] proclaimed the existence of two powers:—

(*a*) The Self-existent God, or θεός, and

(*b*) The Intellect or Word emanating from this, or λόγος. Probably he meant the two forms of God's existence :—

(*a*) As Existing *to* Himself, and

(*b*) As Acting *outside* of Himself;

and therefore this latter would be only an *Attribute;* still some of his mystical expressions, if taken literally, could be made to include the distinct personality of each. When he adopted the Egyptian idea of the threefold existence [alluded-to § 7], he defined the Divine nature as existing in the three manifestations of:—

(*a*) The First-cause [or " Agathon "],

(*b*) The Reason [or " Logos"], and

(*c*) The Soul, or Spirit of the Universe;

---

* Ezekiel i. 10.

† Assyria is an interesting instance of arrested developement. If the empire had not been destroyed by the Medes and Babylonians, about B.C. 625, we might have seen the gradual personification process here also, as the priests had already shown the love of mysticism which generates such accretions.

and with his poetic imagination he sometimes separated and personified these metaphysical abstractions. This doctrine of Reason, or Word, or Wisdom, called by its Greek name "Logos," had, as will be seen, an important effect in the corruptions of Christianity.*

§ 17. After his death his disciples personified these three original principles as three gods united with each other by a mysterious and ineffable generation.

III.—JEWISH AND ALEXANDRIAN WRITERS.

The " Wisdom of Solomon."

§ 18. After the conquests by Alexander the Great, the system of Plato was planted at Alexandria. We also learn from Josephus that a number of Jews were settled there by the Ptolemies, among whom were some who devoted themselves to religion and philosophy. These latter became acquainted with Platonism; and the Apocryphal "Wisdom of Solomon", written in Greek about B.C. 150, bears traces of this. Thus —

> ix. 1, "God made all things by His Word and ordained "man by Wisdom", and

> xviii. 15, "Word leaped down from heaven as a fierce "man of war to punish the Egyptians".

Here is a Trinity of God, Word, and Wisdom. Probably

---

* Gibbon, the historian, says — "The divine sanction which the "Apostle had bestowed on the fundamental principle of the theology "of Plato, encouraged the learned proselytes of the second and third "centuries to admire and study the writings of the Athenian sage, who "had thus marvellously anticipated one of the most surprising disco- "veries of the Christian revelation" (Decline and Fall, chap. xxi.). Whether this study was of benefit to Christianity will be shown in the following pages. "Discoveries" was not the right word to use ; but perhaps Gibbon was only covertly sneering at the whole.

the "word" and "wisdom" had been only used by the earliest Jewish writers as synonyms, in order to avoid using the same expression twice: we have many instances of this in the Old Testament; but they were taken literally as referring to *three* agencies. They were not yet *personified* among the Jews, but only used *poetically*, as shown in the second instance above; nevertheless this was a further step towards the subsequent introduction of the Trinitarian hypothesis into Christian teaching.

Philo.

§ 19. Philo was one of the Jews of Alexandria, living B.C. 25; he was familiar with Platonism, and with the Hindoo ideas brought back by the Greeks after Alexander's campaigns.

§ 20. The Septuagint translation of the Old Testament, from Hebrew to Greek, for the use of the Alexandrine Jews, having rendered the Hebrew "Dabar" (word) by the same term which Plato had allegorised—"Logos"— Philo applied the Platonic meaning of that word [now crystallised into a separate personality by the Platonists] to this version of the Old Testament and to the "Wisdom "of Solomon"; and explained them by saying that the Self-existent or Supreme God was too ineffable to have anything to do with Matter; and that therefore it was His Word or Logos [then first called a separate being], which created the world, and that man was formed in the image of the Logos.

§ 21. His writings are obscure, and not always consistent: sometimes he mentions *two* Gods, and sometimes *three;* thus—"There is a Supreme God, and a second God "who is His Logos", and "there are three orders, of

" which the best is the *Being-that-is*, and He has two
" ancient Powers near Him, one called 'God' and one
" called 'Lord,' and the middle Divinity sometimes pre-
" sents to the mind *one* image and sometimes three ".　This
is somewhat mystical, and it shows how the doctrines of
Platonism were used in explaining and illustrating Jewish ideas,
and had thus obtained a footing in Old Testament exegesis.

IV.—THE EVANGELISTS.

§ 22.　We have thus seen how, before the Christian era,
trinitarian doctrines had existed, and had begun to infect
Judaism.

§ 23.　The teaching of Jesus and the Apostles was strictly
and completely Unitarian [as has been shown], and other
views are only mentioned to be disapproved.*

V.—THE GNOSTICS.

§ 24.　The Gnostic philosophy must now be noticed: there
were several sects included in this broad term; but their
principal views were a mixture of Egyptian superstition,
Platonic philosophy, Judaism, Hindoo mysticism, and the

---

* Athanasius, three centuries afterwards, admitted this ; and endeavoured to account for it on the principle that the Jews were so firmly
persuaded that the Messiah was to be nothing more than a man like
themselves, that the Apostles were obliged to use great caution in
divulging the doctrine of the proper divinity of Christ (De Sen-
tentia Dionysii, ed. 1630 : pp. 553-4). Jesus himself, who never
hesitated to oppose the errors of his countrymen, would surely have
announced it if it had been so ; and the result of the insinuation is that
Athanasius charges the Apostles by implication, with a *suppressio veri !*
Other so-called " orthodox " theologians have made similar admissions
about the Unitarianism of the early Church; and have endeavoured to
account for it, with no more success.

theory of opposing good and evil principles derived from the Persians. (11)   They looked upon Matter as intrinsically evil; and held that, God having created seven Æons or beings, one of them was His instrument in creating the World according to His will.

25. The Docetæ [or "Seemers", so-called from their doctrine], one of the Gnostic sects, held that one of the Æons, called "Christ", put on the shape of a man, but that he was not clad in real human flesh and blood, and consequently he suffered in appearance only.   This first corruption of Christianity took place in the time of the Apostles; and was expressly condemned by John,* by whom stress is laid on the fact that Christ came *in the flesh.*

§ 26. The Gnostic doctrines unfortunately gained root in the Christian Church of the second century, partly from the proneness of the Greek converts towards subtle speculations or "gnosis" (1 Cor. viii. 2); and partly because these opinions gave more supposed dignity to Jesus, and thus helped to obviate their objection to receive as Master one who had been executed as a malefactor.   The Apostle Paul wrote of the Crucifixion as a great obstacle to the reception of the Gospel even in his time; yet he did not seek to hide it, but wrote to the Corinthians [Greeks of an important and polished city] that he was determined "not to know " anything" among them " save Jesus Christ, and him " crucified ".†

* John 1. 14: "And the word became flesh and dwelt among us." 1 John iv. 2 and 3 : " Every spirit which confesseth that Jesus Christ " is come in the flesh is of God ; and every spirit which confesseth not " Jesus is not of God : and this is the spirit of the antichrist, whereof " ye have heard that it cometh ; and now it is in the world already." —*Revised Version.*

† 1 Cor. ii. 2.

§ 27. After his time, however, to meet the objection, some Christian teachers began gradually to exalt the personality of Jesus; and instead of being only a *man* of like nature with ourselves, he was believed to have been possessed by the Logos, not to the exclusion of, but in addition to his humanity.   As the "logos" with these Christians only meant the influence or grace of God, and was not yet deified, they escaped the contradiction which the present doctrine of the " *Double-nature* " [*i.e.*, of two inconsistent elements] presents. This " possession " by the Logos helped them, in dealing with Greeks, to show the superior antiquity of Christianity to Hellenic philosophy—as the Logos had existed before the World, and the Logos, according to these Gnostics, was Christ.

§ 28. Some writers are of opinion that the doctrine of the Miraculous Conception grew up about this time, for the purpose of meeting the objection mentioned by Paul.   After the early chapters in Matthew and Luke there is no allusion to it in the New Testament, even when, if true, it might have been useful for argument ; and it contradicts the genealogies tracing Jesus' descent through Joseph as his father, which were probably derived from documents, while the doctrine could only be from hearsay.

§ 29. There are also traces of the increasing tendency to call the Saviour more exclusively by *titles*, *e.g.* "the Son ", " the Christ ", instead of by his own proper name—Jesus, which raised their conception of him, from simple human and personal relations with brethren, to some higher plane of being.   This vague and indiscriminate use of language, arising at first from genuine love and veneration of Jesus ; a false shame [§ 26]; and their leaning to Oriental mysticism were the main causes of the innovations at this time : afterwards, as will be shown, sacerdotalism became a potent influence in the further addition of doctrines.

VI.—INTRODUCTION OF THE LOGOS INTO CHRISTIANITY.
Justin Martyr.

§ 30. Justin Martyr, A.D. 150, the next link in the chain of developement, is an instance of the proneness of converts to blend their previous religion with the one they take up. He was a Greek by birth, and a Platonist, *i.e.*, a Trinitarian heathen, before he embraced the Christianity that he helped to defend and spread, and also, unhappily, from his fondness for mysticism and far-fetched typical illustrations, to corrupt.

§ 31. He wrote much about the Logos, with many different meanings, but principally as the Supreme Reason, an attribute of God, which had been afterwards given-off as an emanation, and made into a separate person or inferior God; and he was probably among the first in the Christian Church who sought to identify it with the Creative Jehovah and with the God who appeared to Abraham, Jacob, Moses, and elsewhere, in the Old Testament. (III)

§ 32. He says this Logos became flesh in Christ ; and that as an Attribute of God, it was eternal, *i.e.* without beginning, while the Son was not. He clearly held the inferiority of Jesus in his nature: he speaks of his distinctness from God, and calls him "the next in rank" and "next after God", (IV) and he represents the Christians of his time as offering prayer "*to* God *through* Jesus Christ". (v)

§ 33. He does not definitely mention the Holy Spirit except as an influence or mode of working; and in fact, he [as well as others of the early "Fathers"] confounds the

Logos with the Spirit (VI) in a manner which would have
been shocking to the theologians of the Nicene creed.

§ 34. From what can be gathered out of his vague statements, he appears at other times to have held a *Duality:* he
expressly contends for *two* Gods and *two* Lords; and quotes
the "us" of Gen. iii. 22, the double mention of the word
"Lord" in Gen. xix. 24, and the poetic manner in which
Wisdom is personified and made to speak in Proverbs viii.
22, as proofs.   He says they are "numerically distinct", and
are "*two* in number". (VII)   Thus though he was more than
a Unitarian, *i.e.* a believer in the simple one-ness of God
and in the human-ness of Jesus, he was not a Trinitarian;
and the " Fathers " between him and Hippolytus were not
Trinitarians either.

VII.—THE WORD "TRINITY" USED BY CHRISTIANS.
Theophilus.

§ 35. Theophilus, A.D. 169, a Greek convert was the
first Christian who used the word "Trinity".   He makes a
τριας or Trinity consisting of God, His logos, and His
wisdom; and he joins the words "God, the word, wisdom,
man" (VIII) in a manner which shows he did not hold the
modern Trinitarian doctrine: indeed, his Trinity is one of
Attributes, rather than of Persons; and he says expressly,
" The True God [*i.e.* the Father] is alone to be wor-
" shipped ". (IX)

VIII.—CONTROVERSY ABOUT THE GENERATION OF THE
SON.
Irenæus.

§ 36. Irenæus, A.D. 177, a Greek of Asia Minor, makes a
distinction between the Son and the "One only True

"God". (x)   He also clearly asserts the supremacy of God the Father. (xi)

§ 37. He believed the Logos dwelt in Jesus instead of the ordinary human soul; and says that he suffered in his *whole* nature, (xii) in opposition to the Gnostics.

§ 38. He is not clear about the "Generation of the Son", and refuses to attempt to define it, as impossible. (xiii) This was wise; and it would have been well for the world if others had shown the same modesty.

Tertullian and Clement.

§ 39. Tertullian, A.D. 192, a Latin of Carthage, on the contrary, laid it down that the Logos having existed *from Eternity* with the Father, *i.e.* as a part or Attribute of Him, became the Son *in Time* (xiv): thus holding the Pre-existence, but denying the Eternity of the Son.

§ 40. He says the Son is God in his nature, because born of a God, *i.e. begotten,* thereby applying the idea of animal-generation in place of the metaphysical procession.* His teaching caused much dispute and unhappiness among the people, who had been taught the strict Unity of God; and when charged with teaching a *Plurality* of Gods, he explained by saying the Father is a Monarch, or Single Source-of-being, and the Son and Spirit are His subordinates or agents included in His sovreignty (xv); and he

---

* The doctrine, of one God having other Gods as relatives [*e.g.* the God ZEUS being one of the sons of the God CHRONOS, and having as sons the Gods ARES, APOLLO, &c., and as daughters ATHENA and others] was common enough to the surrounding Pagans, who would therefore not be shocked at the idea of our Heavenly Father, who "is " a Spirit " [or " *is Spirit* "—John iv. 24], *begetting progeny* similarly to His creatures.

explains John x. 30, "I and the Father are one" as a one-ness of affection. (XVI)

§ 41. He has left three Creeds, all of which assert the distinct supremacy of the Father. We give one :—
" We believe in one only God, omnipotent, Maker of the
" world ; and his son Jesus Christ, born of the virgin
" Mary, crucified under Pontius Pilate, raised from the
" dead the third day, received into the heavens, now sitting
" at the right hand of the Father and who shall come to
" judge the living and the dead through the resurrection of
" the flesh". (XVII)
It will be noticed that he makes the *Father* the *Maker of the World*, in opposition to Gnosticism. Altogether this creed is not unlike the so-called "Apostles' creed", which is Unitarian.

§ 42. Clement, A.D. 215, a Greek of Alexandria, held much the same opinions as Tertullian. He only uses the word "Trinity" once, and then it is to denote the bond of Christian graces, Faith, Hope, and Charity. (XVIII)

Hippolytus.

§ 43. Hippolytus, A.D. 220, a Greek, Bishop of Porto, near Rome, believed in a Trinity, not a co-equal three, but with strict subordination of the two latter to the First. He explains John x. 30, by saying that Jesus used the same expression towards the Disciples (XIX); and he decidedly ascribes no personality to the Holy Spirit (XX).

IX.—LOGICAL RE-ACTION.
The " Patri-passians."

§ 44. The departure from the simplicity and truth of the Gospel, in the doctrine of the deification of Jesus, now

began to produce its natural results.   Some [the " Patri-
passians ", Sabellius, and others] accepted it, and endeavoured to reconcile it with the Unity of God; while others,
like Origen, opposed it, and preached the humanity of
Christ as recorded in the Gospels.

§ 45. The first-named school arose in the time of Tertullian: they did not accept his explanation [§ 40]; and,
while clinging to the error of the deity of Jesus, refused to
admit a Plurality of Gods.   They therefore supposed that
the Father for the purpose of revealing Himself had "pos-
" sessed " Jesus; and they claimed that this view preserved
the " Unity of God", while it "honoured the Son"; but
their opponents [among whom was Tertullian, from whom
we derive most of our information about them] accused
them of teaching that *the Father had suffered;* hence the
name " Patri-passian".   We have then the two doctrines
before us:—

(a)	(b)
On the one side the Plurality of Tertullian.	On the other Patri-passian-ism.

This antithesis stated in detail would be:—

(a)	(b)
That Jesus having been assumed to be God: if there were another God—*i.e.* the Father —*then there were two Gods.*	That Jesus having been assumed to be God, as before: if there were only *one* God—then the Father and Jesus must be the same person; — *therefore the Heavenly Father suffered on the Cross.*

Praxeas is named as having held this latter shocking
doctrine

Origen.

§ 46. Origen, A.D. 230, a Greek of Alexandria, born not of Pagan but Christian parentage, was the ablest opponent at this time of the Trinitarian doctrines which had invaded Christianity, although he himself was not free from the mysticism and fanciful interpretation then current.

§ 47. He opposed the Patri-passians, saying—"We do not " hold with them, but rather believe his own declaration, " 'The Father who sent me is greater than I '". (XXI)

§ 48. He asserts—"the Father and Son are two [separate] " things in essence, but one in consent and will": he explains John x. 30 similarly to Tertullian [§ 40], and illustrates it from Acts iv. 32: "And the multitude of them that believed " were of one heart and soul ". (XXII)

§ 49. He says—"the Father is alone Good, and greater " than him who was sent " (XXIII); and he expressly directs prayer to be addressed—"not even to Christ, but to the " God and Father of the universe alone ". (XXIV)

§ 50. This it will be seen is not very different from the teaching of Jesus himself; but it did not escape condemnation by Councils held at Constantinople A.D. 553 and 680; which might possibly have condemned even Jesus himself, as not sufficiently orthodox for that time.

Sabellius.

§ 51. Sabellius, A.D., 255, of Ptolemais in Egypt, endeavoured to reconcile the doctrine of the *Deity of Christ* with the *Unity of God* by supposing that God existed in one person, but in three *relations:*—

(*a*) In Creation and giving the Law,
(*b*) In the person of Jesus, and
(*c*) In the elevating influence called the Holy Spirit;

and that these were not separate persons, but only different methods of revealing Himself. He taught that Jesus was the manifestation of God, having the Power of God hypostatized [or fixed] in him during his abode on earth, but this *"possession"* was transient, not permanent: "it " neither existed before his incarnation nor since his death, " having returned again to God ".*

X.—Return to Mysticism.

Arius.

§ 52. Arius, A.D. 320, a Presbyter of a church in Alexandria, preached strongly against the errors of Sabellianism, but in so doing fell into the opposite extreme. He offended his Bishop by reproaching him for Sabellianism, and was banished A.D. 321. He took refuge in Syria, where his opinions soon spread, as also on the north coast of Africa. Eusebius of Nicomedia joined him ; and his followers are hence often called "Eusebians."

§ 53. He and his followers claimed, amid their persecutions, that their doctrines were not new, but merely a return to the old and proper idea of the *subordination* of the Son to the Father (xxv); and they appealed to the ancient traditions in support of them. (xxvi)

§ 54. The characteristic doctrines of his followers were—

* It will be noticed that of the two attempts to harmonise the extraneous doctrine of the Deity of Jesus with the Bible doctrine of the Unity of God : the first, by the " Patri-passians ", made the Heavenly Father *identical in person* with Jesus; and the second, by Sabellius, sought to bridge the insuperable difficulty by supposing that the Heavenly Father *possessed the person* of Jesus. This latter doctrine is true in the sense in which God "possesses", in greater or less degree, all His children who in Him "live and move and have " their being "—Acts xvii. 28—but not in any other sense.

" that the Son was produced out of nothing, and was not of
" the *same substance* [even if of a *similar substance*] with the
" Father". Also, "that there was a period when the Son *did*
" *not* exist", *i.e.* when God alone existed: the order of creation
being that God firstly created His Son, and afterwards the
World with sun, moon, &c.; and hence as *time* could only
commence after there was something to measure it by [*i.e.*
the revolution of the heavenly bodies], therefore the Son was
created *before time*, but *not from eternity.** Arius did not
wish to lower the dignity of Jesus, but to give him the
greatest honour which any created being could have *after
God* his Creator. (xxvii)

XI.—Authoritative Theology.
(1) *Council of Nicæa.*

§ 55. The spread of Arianism was much opposed by the
Bishop of Alexandria, and the dispute grew so bitter
between the theologians that the Emperor Constantine found
it necessary to interfere. He summoned a General Council
of the Church, which met in June, A.D. 325, at a place
called Nicæa, in Bithynia. The Emperor was present in
person, and his favourite Hosius presided. The number of
Bishops was 318, and the duration of the Council rather
more than two months. It is doubtful if Constantine were
qualified to understand metaphysical discussions ; it is possible that a well-timed hint, that Eusebius, one of the Arian
leaders, had recently assisted his political rival, was sufficient
for his decision. (xxviii)

§ 56. After much disputation and some compulsion (xxix),

---

* This was a step farther than Tertullian, who made the *logos,
from eternity* become the *Son, in time.*

the opponents of Arius succeeded in gaining the majority of votes; and they proceeded to draw up a formula which should exclude the Arians. This was the nucleus of the famous "Nicene Creed" which is now used in the Roman Catholic mass, and likewise in the communion service of the Church of England. The clause — "consubstantialem Patri"—"being of one substance with the Father"—was expressly intended to exclude the Arians.* The creed [see Appendix] was adopted *"by authority"*; and Arius and several of the Bishops who had opposed its adoption were banished. This was the sad beginning of State persecution by professing followers of Jesus, which has since led to such lamentable results in the Christian Church.

§ 57. The term "consubstantial" was afterwards explained by Athanasius, one of the disputants at the Council,† to mean—thát Christ being God by birth, *i.e.* descended or begotten by a God, was of the *same* [*i.e. Divine*] *nature* as God; in the same manner as all men, being descended from human parents, have the same [*i.e.* human] nature. Thus the great spiritual fact, which underlies all Trinities —that the Heavenly Father has not left His children without a witness, either (*a*) by raising up one of them to speak *outwardly* to the human soul, or (*b*) by the voice of conscience *within*—was covered up by these materialistic ideas. It is the mission of the Unitarian Church to remove these latter, and to restore Christian doctrine to its primitive purity and simplicity.

* The Greek word for *consubstantial* is ὁμο-ούσιος—homo-ousios ; and for the Semi-Arian view, of a *similar* substance, is ὁμοι-ούσιος—homoi-ousios; and this difference of the letter *i* or iota (ι) gave rise to the sneer of the profane.

† This is the Athanasius, afterwards Archbishop of Alexandria, to whom the Trinitarian Creed, mentioned about A.D. 500, was ascribed.

§ 58. The term "consubstantial" soon came to mean *individual identity*, and also equality; and the mode of defence changed correspondingly. Whereas, in opposition to the charge of Plurality:—

(*a*) Tertullian had asserted the inferiority and *subordination* of the Son ;

(*b*) it was now said that "as the persons were of *one* " individual essence, there was only *one* object of " supreme worship ".

[*Council of Chalcedon.*]

§ 59. The Council held at Chalcedon, a century afterwards, A.D. 451, authorised the doctrine of the *Double-nature of Christ;* and theologians began then to say that the Son, as God, was co-equal to the Father ; and, as Man, was inferior to the Father.

(2) *Council of Constantinople.*

§ 60. The Creed as settled at the Council of Nicæa only mentioned the Holy Spirit in general terms: the clause was —"and in the Holy Spirit"—which might mean a person or an influence; and as many interpreted the creed in a di-theistic manner, the Council held at Constantinople, A.D. 381, added the clause—"who with the Father and the Son together is " worshipped and glorified ". This was, as Mosheim says, " the finishing touch"; although other additions to the Creed were made later.

§ 61. The Creeds called the "APOSTLES' CREED" and the "NICENE" CREED, as now contained in the Prayer-book appointed to be used in the Church of England, are given in the Appendix, preceded by PAUL'S CREED as contained in 1 Cor. viii. 6. The additions and omissions of the "Nicene", as compared with the "Apostles'", are worthy of study.

§ 62. In the middle of the fifth century the Doxology was altered by Flavian, a Monk of Antioch, from :—

"Glory be *to* the Father *through* the Son *in* the Holy Spirit," to :—

"Glory be *to* the Father, *to* the Son, and *to* the Holy Spirit."*

§ 63. The Creed commonly called "of Saint Athanasius" appeared about the sixth century. It does not come within the limits of this brief account, but it is interesting as showing the difficulties which are the inevitable result of departure from the simplicity of the Gospel.† And from that time till now there has been almost continual difference among the so-called "Orthodox" themselves‡ about the Trinity and its co-related doctrines; and at the present day it is instructive to note how all thoughtful preachers avoid it, and how widely those who attempt differ in their explanations. It has been shown to be not a part of Christianity ;

* It is interesting to compare these later developements with Paul's doxologies, *e.g.* last verse of Epistle to Romans, ". . . . to the only "wise God, through Jesus Christ, to whom be the glory for ever". Epistle to Philippians iv. 20 : "Now unto our God and Father be "the glory for ever and ever". See also the manner in which he distinguishes between "God our Father" and "the Lord Jesus Christ " in the commencements of his various Epistles.

† Archbishop Tillotson, in a letter to Bishop Burnet from "Lam- "beth House, October 23rd, 1694," says of this creed, "I wish we "were well rid of it;" and the refusal of the English bishops to sanction its omission was the cause of the disruption of the American Episcopalians. (Yates' "Vindication", 1850, p. 318. He refers to Sparks' Letters on the American Episcopalian Church, Letter III.)

‡ See Gibbon III., pp. 238-9, for quotation from Hilary of Poitiers.

and its developement has now been traced.   All through
this period of developement there had been protests made by
those who wished to preserve the truth of the Gospel from
the innovations; but they were gradually overborne, until at
length, when the innovators were strong enough, they called
other Christians "Heretics", and persecuted them.   The
"Truth as it is in Jesus" existed before the accretions; and
will be brighter once more when, as it may be hoped, men
will again be content to follow *him* as their Master, instead
of the ecclesiastics who have formulated Ceremonies and
dictated Creeds.

§ 64. We may derive an *analogy* from the science of
Arithmetic : History, *i.e.* the relation of events, assigning to
each cause its contributing value, may be likened to an
operation in Subtraction, *i.e.* a finding-out of the various
items contributing to any given result.   After performing
the operation, the calculator may, in order to test its
correctness, work the sum backwards-way; and, adding the
items together, ascertain if the original amount be arrived at.

§ 65. This "working the sum backwards-way" may help
us now to understand how the simple teachings of Jesus
have become so added-to; and we may say: given the
items, we can find the amount; given the causes, we can
foresee the result.   Thus considering :—

> (*a*) The glowing Love to the Master who had brought
> life and immortality to light, and had shown such
> sublime self-sacrifice all through his life,
> (*b*) The natural Instinct to add to the dignity of any
> man held in high estimation,*

---

* *E.g.* HERAKLES in Heathen Mythology, and "Saints" in
more recent times.

(*c*) The Desire to present the gospel in an acceptable form to the heathens, and the false Shame of owning a "crucified Christ",

(*d*) The Superstitions of the Egyptians and the subtle Speculations of the Greeks in the city [Alexandria], which was unfortunately the centre of influence at the time, and

(*e*) The accumulating Force of superstitions when once admitted—

we could predict a gradual corruption of doctrine running parallel to a gradual increase of supposed dignity in the conceptions of Jesus;* and give the stages in the Developement:—

(*a*) The tendency to the *exclusive use* of Titles, "Son of God", "Christ", &c., instead of his own proper name—"Jesus";

(*b*) The doctrine of his Pre-existence as "*Son*";

(*c*) That of his Pre-existence as an *inferior God;*

(*d*) That of his *Eternal* Pre-existence as an inferior God;

(*e*) That of his being *co-equal* with the Heavenly Father;

(*f*) The doctrine of the *personality* of the Holy Spirit as a separate being from the Heavenly Father; and finally

(*g*) That of the deity of the Holy Spirit.

§ 66. It is a painful task to trace in the History of the Church the disputes of theologians in the depth of metaphysical mysticism, so soon as they had departed from the solid ground of Christ's simplicity: it is to be hoped, in

---

* As if any dignities could add to the complete revelation of the Father which he showed !

the increasing love of Bible-reading and the clearer intelligence and deeper reverence of our age, that the Christian
Church may cast off the Pagan philosophy; and, sweeping
away the inherited accretions, come to see the Gospel in
that original purity and beauty which, when fairly and
lovingly presented, will win the world, and bring all nations
to the knowledge and love of Him who is the Father of all.
As a small effort towards that glorious consummation, this
brief statement is submitted to the candid and prayerful
consideration of all reverent and earnest minds.

Christmas, 1881.   H. H. S.

Divisions of the Subject, and Table showing Chronological Developement :—

I.—PAGAN TRINITIES:
 B.C. 700 (1) Egypt, § 7.
  „ 800 (2) India, § 10.
  „ 720 (3) Assyria, § 14.

II.—PHILOSOPHIC THEORIES:
 B.C. 360 Platonism, § 15.

III.—JEWISH AND ALEXANDRINE WRITERS:
 B.C. 150 (1) "Wisdom of Solomon", § 18.
  „ 25 (2) Philo, § 19.

IV.—THE EVANGELISTS, § 22.

V.—THE GNOSTICS, A.D. 50, § 24.

VI.—INTRODUCTION OF "LOGOS":
 A.D. 150 Justin Martyr, § 30.

VII.—THE WORD "TRINITY" USED BY CHRISTIANS:
 A.D. 169 Theophilus, § 35.

VIII.—CONTROVERSY ABOUT GENERATION OF SON:
 A.D. 177 (1) Irenæus, § 36.
  „ 200 (2) Tertullian and Clement, § 39.
  „ 220 (3) Hippolytus, § 43.

IX.—LOGICAL RE-ACTION:
 A.D. 220 (1) Patri-passians, § 44.
  „ 230 (2) Origen, § 46.
  „ 255 (3) Sabellius, § 51.

X.—RETURN TO MYSTICISM:
 A.D. 320 Arius, § 52.

XI.—AUTHORITATIVE THEOLOGY.
 A.D. 325 (1) Council of Nicæa, § 55.
  „ 381 (2) Council of Constantinople, § 60.

Platonising Fathers. (bracket spanning sections VI–IX)

APPENDIX TO PRIZE ESSAY.

PAUL'S CREED, A.D. 57, "To us there is one God, the Father, "of whom are all things, and we unto him; and one Lord, Jesus "Christ, through whom are all things, and we by him."—I. Cor. viii. 6. [See also the commencements of all his Epistles.]

The "APOSTLES' CREED", used circa A.D. 400, in its present form, but in substance dating from the very earliest Christian times.

The NICENE CREED, composed A.D. 325; the portion in curved brackets ( ) was interpolated at the Council of Toledo, in A.D. 589, and was the cause of the split of the Western or Latin branch from the main Greek Catholic Church: the remaining portion in square brackets [ ] had been previously interpolated in A.D. 381 at the Council of Constantinople.

I believe in God
the Father Almighty,
Maker of heaven and earth:

And in Jesus Christ His only Son
our Lord,

Who was conceived
by the Holy Ghost,
Born
of the Virgin Mary,

I believe in one God
the Father Almighty,
Maker of heaven and earth,
And of all things visible and invisible:

And in one Lord Jesus Christ, the only-begotten Son of God,
Begotten of his Father before all worlds,
God of *or from* God, Light of *or from* Light,
Very God of *or from* Very God,
Begotten, not made,
Being of one substance with the Father;
By whom were all things made,
Who for us men and for our salvation came down from heaven,

And was incarnate
by the Holy Ghost
of the Virgin Mary,
And was made man,

Suffered under Pontius Pilate, Was crucified,	And was crucified also for us under Pontius Pilate, He suffered
dead, and buried; He descended into Hell; The third day he rose again from the dead.	and was buried, And the third day he rose again according to the Scriptures,
He ascended into heaven, And sitteth on the right hand of God the Father Almighty; From thence he shall come to judge the quick and the dead	And ascended into heaven, And sitteth on the right hand of the Father. And he shall come again with glory to judge both the quick and the dead: Whose kingdom shall have no end.
I believe in the Holy Ghost;	And I believe in the Holy Ghost, [The Lord and Giver of life, Who proceeded from the Father (and the Son), Who with the Father and Son together is worshipped and glorified, Who spake by the Prophets.]
The Holy Catholic Church;	And I believe one Catholic and Apostolic Church.
The Communion of Saints: The Forgiveness of	I acknowledge one Baptism for the remission of
sins;	sins, And I look for
The Resurrection of the body,	the Resurrection of the dead
And the life everlasting.	And the life of the world to come.

AMEN.

NOTES.

[The writer has availed himself of the scholarship of others for these references.]

I.—The Hindu Pantheon, being Part I. of The Industrial Arts of India, by Dr. Birdwood, C.S.I., London, 1880, pp. 48-9. See also Hibbert Lectures, 1878, by Max Müller, pp. 290-1, about this and about "dual-gods."

II.—Neander; General Church History. Vol. II., p. 47.

III.—Dial. cum Tryphonte ed. Otto, c. 56; see also cc. 57-62; and ed. Thirlby, p. 264.

IV.—Apol. I., p. 63; Otto, c. 32. See also Apol. II., p. 97; Otto, c. 13, and Apol. I. cc. 12 and 13; and Dial., cc. 126-7.

V.—Dial. ed. Par. 1742; Apol. I., pp., 82-3; Otto, cc. 65-7.

VI.—Apol. I., p, 64; Otto, c. 33.

VII.—Dial., p. 222; Thirlby, pp. 413-4; Otto, c. 129.

VIII.—Ad Autol. lib. II., cap. 15.

IX.—Ad Autol. lib. I., cap. 11, lib. II., cap. 35.

X.—Contra Hær. lib. V., cap. 18, § 2; lib. I., cap. 10, § 1.

XI.—Ibid. See I. 22, § 1; III. 6, § 1; III. 8, § 3; IV. 6, § 7; IV. 38, § 3.

XII.—Ibid. III., cc. 16-18.

XIII.—Ibid. II. 28, § 6 and § 8.

XIV.—Adv. Hermog., c. 3.

XV.—Adv. Praxeam, cc. 3-4. See also c. 13.

XVI.—Ibid. c. 22.

XVII.—De Virg. Veland., c. 1. The two others are given in De Præscrip. Hæret. c. 13 and Adv. Prax., c. 2.

XVIII.—Stromata. L. IV., p. 495.

XIX.—Bunsen: Hist. Christian Dogma, ed. Bohn, p. 163.

XX.—Meier: Lehre von der Trinität, I. 88.

XXI.—Contra Cels. VIII. 14.

XXII.—Ibid. VIII. 12.

XXIII.—Comment. in Joan., t. XIII., § 25; Opp., IV. 235-6.

XXIV.—De Orat., § 15; Opp., I. 222-3.

XXV.—Neander.

XXVI.—See his letter to his bishop quoted in Newman's Library of the Fathers, VIII., pp. 96-8.

XXVII.—Neander: Histy., Vol. II., pp. 361-5; Hist. Christian Dogmas, pp. 286-7.

XXVIII.—See Theodoret, lib. I., cap. 20, where Constantine mentions Eusebius as implicated in the cruelty of the tyrant, and complains of his hostile conduct during the civil war. Gibbon.

XXIX.—Neander: Hist. Christian Religion, Vol. II., pp. 377-8.

GENERAL APPENDIX.

ILLUSTRATIONS OF THE TRINITY.

Attempts have been made, in every age since the Trinity was introduced into the list of Christian doctrines, to show its rationality by illustrations. We are of opinion that these all signally fail, and must fail, while the doctrine states that the " Father is Almighty, the Son is Almighty, and the Holy Ghost " is Almighty ; yet there are not three Almighties, but one " Almighty".

It would appear that at a very early period in Church history, the teachers of this doctrine of the Trinity resorted to illustrations. Schaff says, " They found a sort of triad in the universal " law of thesis, antithesis, and synthesis ; in the elements of " syllogism ; in the three persons of grammar ; in the construc- " tion of body, soul, and spirit". . . . " The Holy Trinity, " though the most evident, is yet the deepest of mysteries, and " can be adequately explained by *no* finite and earthly things". —*History of the Christian Church, vol. i., p.* 284.

One of the first illustrations of the Trinity we meet with in history, about the close of the second century—for then the word Trinity appears, but not the Trinity of "three equal " persons"—is as follows : " The three days which preceded " the luminaries are types of the Trinity, of God and His " Word and His Wisdom". We have read of one of the popes ordering a piece of jewellery made to represent the three Gods at work. " While residing in France", wrote a correspondent of the *Times*, " I met a Spanish monk, who, with the appro- " bation of the clergy of the district, was selling a variety " of tracts, intended as hard hits for the Protestants. The most " striking argument used in these papers was, 'That to confirm " 'the faith of unbelievers in the Trinity in Unity, a certain " 'cathedral in Spain (Seville, I believe) could show among its

" ' holy relics three pieces of the flesh of some holy man, which
" ' individually weighed an ounce, and collectively weighed an
" ' ounce ' ; and the writer argued that, as no Protestant church
" could show so convincing a proof of the Trinity in Unity,
" heretics were deprived of a very strong and consoling founda-
" tion for their belief ".

It is said that Horne Tooke once complained to an orthodox
friend of his about the self-contradictory character of the
doctrine. " Not at all contradictory ", said his friend ; "it is
" only like a thing that I have just seen in the street—three men
" riding in one cart ". " It would be more to the purpose ",
answered Tooke, "if you had seen one man riding in three carts".

Some authors seriously tell us how the doctrine ceased to be a
mystery to them, by the three chief colours united in one rainbow.
Others tell us how the three faculties of the soul—the understanding, the conscience, and the will—all blending in one man,
illustrate to them the Trinity. Some, like John Wesley, speak
of the difficulty being no greater to them than three candles in
one room blending into one light. They might as well speak of
three measures of water making one larger measure, and fondly
believe this is an illustration of the Trinity. None of these really
touch the question as it is put before us in the creeds of the
Churches. "The Father is perfect God, the Son is perfect God,
" and the Holy Ghost is perfect God ; and yet there are not three
" Gods, but one God". No illustration of the blending of finite
things bears a particle of analogy to three distinct Almighty and
Infinite Beings making one Almighty and Infinite Being. This
is the doctrine of the Church ; and it is so defined by Dr. Wallis :
" According to the Word of God, the sacred Trinity of the
" Father, Son, and Holy Ghost are so distinguished that the
" Father is not the Son or the Holy Ghost, the Son is not the
" Father or the Holy Ghost, neither is the Holy Ghost the
" Father or the Son, but so united and intimately one that they
" are all one God ".

Professor Stuart, in the *Biblical Repository* for April, 1835,
says :—" Who will venture to say that any of the definitions
" heretofore given of personality in the Godhead, in itself con-
" sidered—I mean such definitions as have their basis in the
" Nicene or Athanasian Creed—are intelligible and satisfactory

" to the mind? At least I can truly say that I have not been
" able to find them, if they do in fact exist ; nor, so far as I
" know, has anyone been able, by any commentary on them, to
" render them clear and satisfactory. If I say in words that
" Christ and the Spirit are God, and very God, and say this ever
" so strongly or so often, and yet assign to them attributes or a
" condition which, after all, makes them dependent, and repre-
" sents them as derived and originated, then I am in fact no
" real believer in the doctrine of true equality among the persons
" of the Godhead, or else I use expressions out of their lawful
" and accustomed sense, and lose myself amid the sound of
" words, while things are not examined and defined with scru-
" pulous care and accuracy".

We are all acquainted with the paradoxes attributed to Lord
Bacon on this matter; absurd as they may appear, they are but
the simple statement of the difficulties. He observes that
a Christian believer in the Trinity " believes three to be one and
" one to be three ; a father not to be older than his son ; a son
" to be equal with his father ; and one proceeding from both to
" be equal with both. He believes in three persons in one nature,
" and three natures in one person. He believes a virgin to be a
" mother of a son, and that very son of hers to be her Maker.
" He believes Him to have been shut up in a narrow room whom
" heaven and earth could not contain. He believes Him to
" have been born in time who was and is from everlasting. He
" believes Him to have been a weak child, carried in arms, who
" is the Almighty ; and Him once to have died who only hath
" life and immortality in himself".

After this, we cannot help thinking that Cardinal Wiseman had
sufficient grounds for making the following remarkable statement:
—" Who will pretend to say that he can, by any stretch of his
" imagination or of his reasoning, see it possible how three
" persons in one God can be but one Godhead? If the contra-
" diction—the apparent contradiction—to the laws of nature, as
" usually observed and understood by us, is to be the principle
" for rejecting a notion clearly laid down in Scripture, and if the
" Eucharist, which is more clearly laid down than the Trinity,
" is to be rejected on that ground, how is it possible, for a
" moment, to support the doctrine of the Trinity? The very

F

" idea is itself, at first sight, apparently repugnant to the law
" of number, and no mathematical, no speculative reasoning,
" will ever show how it possibly can be. You are content, then,
" to receive that important mystery, shutting your eyes to its
" difficulties".

From such statements as these, we are tempted to ask, Does
anyone believe this doctrine ? Men and women may " receive ",
or sing, or say certain things about God being "three", God
being "born", God "dying", &c., but does any rational and
intelligent person believe these things ? Archbishop Secker
says, " Let any proposition be delivered to us, as coming from
" God, or from man, we can believe it no further than we under-
" stand it : and, therefore, if we do not understand it at all, we
" cannot believe it at all".

We are not inclined to believe, in this more enlightened and
rational age—in which men are conjured to "think for themselves",
to "prove all things", to be "fully persuaded in their own minds",
and to "render a reason for the hope that is in them"—that they
are likely to subscribe to the sentiment that "ignorance is the
" mother of devotion", or that faith in these mysteries or contradictions is more acceptable to God than a "reasonable service".
Advocates of religion are now disposed, more than ever, in
commending religion, to dwell on its " sweet reasonableness ";
and this, among other things, will certainly compel Christian
teachers to get rid of the most unthinkable or contradictory of
all theological propositions—the doctrine of the Trinity.

THE TRINITY A SOURCE OF MENTAL CONFUSION.

IT is said that when St. Augustine was writing his discourse
on the Trinity, he strolled by the seaside in meditation. There
he saw a child digging a hole in the sand, and then attempting
to fill it with sea water. In answer to the student, the child said
he intended to empty the great deep. "Impossible", said
Augustine. "Not more impossible", said the child, "than for
" you to explain the Trinity". These are the kind of tales which
men tell to save themselves from giving any explanation of a
doctrine which they are taught to say is fundamental in religion.

The late Archbishop Sumner, in his sermon on "The Duty " of Acquainting Ourselves with God", says :—" Here, however, " I am scarcely less foiled than before, if I attempt to form to " myself any distinct idea of this mysterious Godhead. I am " not able to comprehend, with any clearness, the union of " Person, and the distinction of Person, represented in Scripture. " I am at a loss to conceive how the nature of God should be " incorporated with that of man in the incarnation of Jesus " Christ. I cannot understand the operation of the Holy Spirit " upon the human heart ; much less can I explain that opera- " tion in the extent and degree which Scripture asserts, and " still leave room for the developement of individual character, " which the same Scripture obliges me to recognise. A very " short inquiry is sufficient to convince me, that if I am not to " be at peace till I am acquainted with God in all these mysteries " of his nature, I must sit down in despair ".

We are disposed to ask, what command or injunction could this dignitary point out, in the religion of Christ, that made it incumbent on him to believe in a union and distinction of persons in the Godhead, that was so perplexing? We have referred to the confession of Dr. Hey, a Trinitarian, who says on the Trinity: " My understanding is involved in perplexity, my con- " ceptions bewildered in the thickest darkness. I confess and " proclaim my confusion in the most unequivocal manner ". Similar is the language of the learned Jeremy Taylor, in a sermon before the University of Dublin,—that " if you go about " to speak of, and to understand, the mysterious Trinity, and do " it by words and names of man's invention, you will in the end " find your understanding, like St. Peter's on Mount Tabor, at " the Transfiguration—you may build three tabernacles in your head, and talk something, but you will know not what".

We offer but one quotation more ; the words are those of Bishop Beveridge :—" I cannot set myself to think of the Trinity, " or to screw up my thoughts a little concerning it, but I imme- " diately lose myself as in a trance or ecstacy ". How widely different are these assertions from certain others, which we are disposed to think more nearly approach the truth and the sim- plicity of a religion which was level to the understanding of " the " common people " and which " they heard gladly " ! Our Lord says, "The poor have the Gospel preached to them"; and it is not uncommon now to hear the words, "The wayfaring men, "though fools, shall not err therein". Such passages imply that we have in Christianity a religion that meets the mental capacities and the wants of the labourer and the artizan. Dr. Parr, the distinguished scholar and divine, places this fact in its proper light when he says:— "Christianity is a religion intended for general use: it "appeals to the common feelings of our nature, and never "clashes with the unbiassed dictates of our reason. We may "therefore rank it among the beneficial tendencies, as well as "the peculiar evidences, of such a religion, that the Author of it "abstained from all abstruse speculations". Endless is the testimony, that the Christian religion is not a mass of riddles and mysteries, but a simple thing, intelligible to the humblest intellect.

We have seen that the doctrine of the Trinity is said to "perplex the understanding"; "bewilder the mind"; we cannot "comprehend it"; "when thinking of it, I lose myself as in "a trance or ecstacy"; "it is strange and unaccountable"; "it is the mystery of mysteries"; "seemingly incredible"; "it contradicts our reason"; "it makes us use words without "meaning". Such are the exclamations of learned and devout men who say they believe it. Is it possible, we ask, that they are contemplating a doctrine of that Gospel which "the poor "had preached to them", and "the common people heard gladly", when they thus speak? Certainly not. The schoolmen of the Church have invented, or imported, this view of our heavenly Father, and so done a great injury to the religion of Christ. It was in view of this perplexing theme, the Trinity, that Dr. Watts, in his last days, expressed himself, in his Solemn Address to God, as "embarrassed and bewildered":—

"Dear and blessed God, hadst Thou told me plainly in any "single text, that the Father, Son, and Holy Spirit, are three "real distinct persons in Thy divine nature, I had never suffered "myself to be so bewildered in so many doubts, nor embarrassed "with so many strong fears of assenting to the mere inventions of "men, instead of divine doctrine; but I should have humbly "and immediately accepted Thy words, so far as it was possible

" for me to understand them, as the only rule of my faith. Or
" hadst Thou been pleased so to express and include this proposi-
" tion in the several scattered parts of thy book from whence my
" reason and my conscience might with ease find out, and with
" certainty infer, this doctrine, I should have joyfully employed
" all my reasoning powers, with their utmost skill and activity,
" to have found out this inference, and engrafted it into my soul ".

THE TRINITY A HINDRANCE TO THE SPREAD OF CHRISTIANITY.

IT is well known to those who enter upon missionary work
that the doctrine of the Trinity presents an almost insuperable
difficulty in the effort to make converts of Jews, Mahometans,
Parsees, and others. A Japanese once said, " What a contempt
" you must have of our understanding if we are expected to
" receive instruction like this ". Five times a day the Mahometan
repeats, " There is no God but one God," as a kind of protest
against the theory of a Triune Deity. The well educated
Mahometan tells the Christian missionary that the doctrine of
the Trinity is neither in the Old Testament nor the New, but is
an after-thought grafted upon the primitive Monotheistic creed
which Christ himself taught. Of the intelligent Hindoos, the
late Rev. Rowland Williams (who made Hindoo mythology a
special study) is compelled to acknowledge that Christianity, in
its prevalent form, can never win the general assent of the
Oriental mind, and that only the simple religious ideas and precepts of the Gospel—the Fatherhood of God, the brotherhood
of man, the grand sentiments which harmonise with the intuitive
moral judgment—can exercise long and lasting influence upon
the Hindoo race.

In addition to the difficulties with Mahometans and Pagans, it
is scarcely necessary to repeat the thrice-told tale of the absolute
repugnance of the Jews to the theory of a three-fold Deity. We
know there are some controversialists reckless enough to say
that the Jews were once Trinitarians and may be so again.
This was not the view of Bishop Beveridge, who writes, " The
" Jews have had the law above three thousand years, and the

"prophets above two thousand years, yet to this day they could "never make the Trinity an article of their faith". And Bishop Bloomfield says, in reference to some who hold that the Jews once believed in the Trinity—"I confess that I am not prepared "to go to the full length of these positions. I think it in the "highest degree probable that the Jews expected a Messiah who "would be a sharer in the divine nature, but not one who should "be equal with God".

The following lines, the composition of a Jew, fully illustrate this position :—

> When thou canst wash the Ethiopian white,
> Govern the winds, or give the sun more light,
> Cause by thy word the mountain to remove,
> Control the seas, or hurl the bolts of Jove,—
> Then hope (but not till then) to turn the Jews
> To Christian doctrines and to Christian views.
> For Christian faith, say conscience is thy guide,
> The Jews, for conscience' sake, 'gainst it decide.
> One God thou callest Three, and Three but One ;
> The Jews acknowledge God as One alone.

It would not be difficult to fill pages with the testimony of many learned historians and divines, that the Jews have through all ages believed and upheld the simple and absolute unity of God as one person. They lay great stress on the words, "Jehovah "our God is one Jehovah". When these words are read in their services they emphasise them by repetitions. Canon Farrar, in "Early Days of Christianity", in evidence of the Monotheism of the Jews, gives the following, on the authority of Berachoth : "Thus, as regards Monotheism, we find that in repeating the "Shemâ, or daily prayer, 'Hear, O Israel, the Lord our God is "'one God' (Deut. vi. 4), whosoever prolongs the utterance of "the word ONE (echad), shall have his days and years prolonged "to him". There is similar evidence by Dr. Adam Clarke in his "Commentary", under Deuteronomy vi. 4. The Unity of God is the first and great commandment of Moses, and it is also the first and great commandment of Christ. During the earliest period of Christian history the ablest advocates of Christianity were Jews. At the present time the Jewish race is scattered over all the earth, bearing its testimony to the truth of the doctrine of one God in one person. There is a wide-spead belief that the Mahometans have been raised up by Divine Providence as a protest against the doctrine of the Trinity. Their voice is heard, their worship is felt, over the east of Europe, and in Asia and Africa as well. Some 30 millions of Mahometans are leavening our great empire of India with a Monotheistic theology. It is very questionable if Mahometanism, which has hindered the progress of Christianity in the East, would have had any existence at all in the world had the Church kept to the Monotheism of the New Testament. The Parsees also and the Brahmos constantly proclaim the doctrine of the undivided unity of God. Some years ago when we had a serious difference with the Queen of Oude, and referred in one of our proclamations to the Christian religion, the following reply was issued by her command :—" In the " [Queen of England's] " proclamation " it is written that the Christian religion is true, but no other creed " will suffer oppression ; and that the laws will be observed " towards all. What has the administration of justice to do " with the truth or falsehood of religion ? That religion is true " which acknowledges ONE GOD and knows no other. Where " there are THREE GODS in religion, neither Mussulmans nor " Hindoos, nay, not even Jews, Sun-worshippers, or Fire-" worshippers, can believe it true ".

THE EARLIEST CREEDS.

WE are not about to express any hostility to creeds. They have had, and still have, their good and their evil side. What we wish for as a creed, and bond of union in the Christian Church, is that which expresses the thought of our Lord himself. About the being of God, we all know that Christ reiterates the language of Moses, " The Lord our God is one Lord ". Paul's view also of the nature of God is well known: " To us there is but one " God the Father ". The three creeds which are best known among us now, are the Apostles' Creed, the Nicene, and the Athanasian. It is generally acknowledged that the Apostles'

Creed was the faith of Apostolic times. It is a purely Unitarian creed. The Nicene Creed was not received into the Church until the fourth century. The Athanasian Creed much later. The Rev. W. Gilpin, Prebendary of Salisbury, made a statement some years ago, which few will be inclined to dispute :—
" The Apostles' Creed was composed before any of the subtleties
" of the doctrine of the Trinity were introduced, which tend more
" to create animosity than to promote piety". And, at a
Church Congress held in Plymouth, in 1873, the Rev. B. W. Savile read a paper " On the Athanasian Creed ", in which he says, "We are unable to find a sign of any creed earlier than
"the close of the second century, other than what Scripture
"records. The earliest . . . is in Irenæus, Adv. Hær.
" I. 2. . . . The creed of the Church of Jerusalem, as it
"appears in the Liturgy of St. James, which may possibly be as
" old as the second century, contained only the following words :
"' I believe in one God the Father Almighty, Maker of Heaven
"' and Earth, and in one Lord Jesus Christ, the Son of God '".
Mosheim is certainly in accord with this view, for he writes, of the second century, " The whole Christian system was still com-
" prised in a few precepts and propositions ; nor did the teachers
" publicly advance any doctrines besides those contained in what
"is called the Apostles' Creed ".

Professor Schaff says ("History of the Creeds of Christendom"), that the Apostles' Creed was called by Ante-Nicene fathers, "the rule of faith"; "the rule of truth"; "the apostolic tradi-
" tion"; "the apostolic preaching"; "the symbol of faith ", &c.
" It has", says he, "the fragrance of antiquity and the inesti-
"mable weight of universal consent". Its doctrine of God is simply, "I believe in God the Father Almighty, Maker of heaven
"and earth ; and in Jesus Christ His only Son our Lord".

THE SUFFICIENCY OF THE SCRIPTURES AS A RULE OF FAITH.

AMONG our Protestant Churches we constantly and gladly hear that the best rule of faith is the Bible ; that the Scriptures contain all that is necessary or essential for our salvation. The historian Mosheim remarks, "As long as they (the Scriptures) "were the only rule of faith, religion preserved its native purity; "and in proportion as their decisions were either neglected, or "postponed to the inventions of men, it degenerated from its "primitive and divine simplicity".

Articles of faith may be divided into those which can be stated in the very words of Scripture, and those which cannot be so stated. The Christian Church would suffer no loss but great gain by removing from its creeds and articles all doctrines which are not capable of being expressed by the "wholesome words of "Jesus Christ". And one great obstacle to Christian union would be at once removed if this were done.

If we are at all sincere in our profession, that the faith and practice of pure religion are sufficiently clear in the Sacred Volume and that our appeal for the fundamentals of religion is to the "law and the testimony", "that our faith should stand not "in the wisdom of men, but in the power of God", then we should studiously avoid words and phrases which have no equivalents in the Bible. Hereafter, probably, more attention may be paid to such precepts as the following in speaking of the nature of God : "Ye shall not add unto the word which I command you, neither "shall ye diminish aught from it, that ye may keep the com- "mandments of the Lord your God which I command you this "day".

It is admitted on all sides that the ONE-NESS of God is a doctrine of the Bible ; in fact, there is no doctrine of the Sacred Volume more repeatedly and emphatically stated It is also frankly admitted by learned Trinitarian divines that the doctrine of the *three-ness* of God is one of inference and deduction, not of direct or clear revelation.

Those passages in the New Testament in which the Father is styled ONE, or ONLY GOD, are in number, 17.

Those passages where the Father is styled GOD, *absolutely*, by way of *eminence* and *supremacy*, are in number, 320.

Those passages where he is styled GOD with peculiar high titles and epithets or attributes, are in number, 105.

Those passages wherein it is declared that *all prayers* and praises ought to be offered to the Father, are in number, 90

Passages wherein the SON is declared, positively and by the

clearest implication, to be *subordinate to the Father, deriving his being from Him, receiving from Him his divine power,* and *acting in all things wholly according to the will of the Father,* are in number, above 300.

Jesus Christ is 85 times called the *Son of Man,* and 70 times called *a man* in the New Testament.

Of 1326 passages in the New Testament wherein the word GOD is mentioned, not one of them expresses, or necessarily implies, a plurality of persons.

Now let us see how the case will stand, by drawing a parallel of like authority from Scripture in favour of the Trinity.

Texts, wherein God is spoken of as three distinct equal persons or Beings, and yet but one Being or person—not one.

Texts, in which God is spoken of as three and yet but one, but affording no authority as to their perfect equality, are in number—one (1 John v. 7). And even this solitary one is excluded as spurious from the Revised Version.

Texts in which Father, Son, and Holy Ghost are mentioned, are in number one (Matt. xxviii. 19). And this text is wholly silent as to the requisite distinction of their perfect equality, and perfect unity.

Is it not almost incredible that, in this amazing and endless controversy, nearly all the evidence which is *direct* and intelligible should appear to stand on one side only ? Looking at the absence of texts in favour of the doctrine of the Trinity, and having regard to the number and weight of those which uphold the Unitarian faith, surely those that seem to give some slight support to Trinitarian doctrines may be said scarcely to appear as dust in the balance. In proof of this we reproduce a moiety of the Scriptural evidence for the UNITY OF GOD.

GOD STYLED ONE.

"Hear, O Israel ! Jehovah, our God, is One Jehovah".—Deut. vi. 4.

"The Holy One of Israel".—2 Kings xix. 22.

"I have not concealed the words of the Holy One".—Job vi. 10.

"O thou Holy One of Israel".—Psalm lxxi. 22.

"And Jehovah shall be King over all the earth : in that day
" shall there be One Jehovah, and his name ONE".—Zech. xiv. 9.

"The Holy One of Israel is our King".—Psalm lxxxix. 18.

"The word of the Holy One of Israel".—Isa. v. 24.

"Great is the Holy One of Israel".—Isa. xii. 6.

"At that day shall a man look to his maker, and his eyes shall
" have respect to the Holy One of Israel".—Isa. xvii. 7.

"And the poor among men shall rejoice in the Holy One of
" Israel".—Isa. xxix. 19.

"Have we not all One Father. Hath not One God created
" us".—Mal. ii. 10.

"For thus saith the Lord God, the Holy One of Israel".—
Isa. xxx. 15.

"But they look not unto the Holy One of Israel, neither seek
" the Lord".—Isa. xxxi. 1.

"To whom then will ye liken me, or shall I be equal? saith
" the Holy One".—Isa. xl. 25.

"And thou shalt rejoice in the Lord, and shalt glory in the
" Holy One of Israel".—Isa. xli. 16.

"The hand of the Lord hath done this, and the Holy One of
" Israel hath created it".—Isa. xli. 20.

"For I am the Lord thy God, the Holy One of Israel".—
Isa. xliii. 3.

"The heathen shall know that I am the Lord, the Holy One
" of Israel".—Ezek. xxxix. 7.

"Art thou not from everlasting, O Lord my God, mine Holy
" One".—Habak. i. 12.

"For I am God, and not man ; the Holy One in the midst of
" thee".—Hosea xi. 9.

"One is your Father who is in Heaven".—Matt. xxiii. 9.

"And Jesus said unto him, Why callest thou me good? There
" is none good but One, that is God".—Mark x. 18.

"I am the Lord, your Holy One, the Creator of Israel, your
" King".—Isa. xliii. 15.

"Thus saith the Lord, the Holy One of Israel, and his Maker".
—Isa. xlv. 11.

"As for our Redeemer, the Lord of Hosts is his name, the
" Holy One of Israel".—Isa. xlvii. 4.

" Thus saith the Lord, thy Redeemer, the Holy One of Israel;
" I am the Lord thy God".—Isa. xlviii. 17.

"And Jesus answered him, the first of all the commandments
" is Hear, O Israel! the Lord our God is One Lord".—
Mark xii. 29.

"And the Scribe said unto him, Well, Master, thou hast said
" the truth ; for there is One God, and there is *none other but he*".
Mark xii. 32.

"We know.........there is none other God but One".—
I Cor. viii. 4.

" To us there is but One God, the Father, of whom are all
" things".—I Cor. viii. 6.

" Now a mediator is not a mediator of one, but GOD IS ONE".
—Gal. iii. 20.

" For there is One God, and one Mediator between God and
" men, the Man Christ Jesus".—I Tim. ii. 5.

"One God and Father of all who is above all".—Eph. iv. 6.

" Thou believest there is One God, thou doest well".—
James ii. 19.

It must be evident to every person, from the foregoing
passages, as well as from some of the following texts, that
God the Father, in contra-distinction to Jesus Christ, is the *one*,
only, *alone*, *unequalled*, and *true* God. Jesus Christ in solemn
prayer to his Father, said :

" This is life eternal, that they may know THEE, THE ONLY
" TRUE GOD, and Jesus Christ whom thou hast sent".—John
xvii. 3.

"And Hezekiah prayed before the Lord and said, O Lord God
" of Israel.........thou art the God, even thou alone".—2 Kings
xix. 15.

"That men may know that thou, whose name *alone* is
" Jehovah, art the most high over all the earth".—Psalm lxxxiii. 18.

" For thou art great and doest wondrous things : thou art God
" alone".—Psalm lxxxvi. 10.

"Thou shalt have none other Gods but me".—Exodus xx. 3.

"Thou art Jehovah, even thou *only*".—Isa. xxxvii. 20.

" I am the Lord, and there is none else, there is no God
" beside me".—Isa. xlv. 5.

" Unto thee it was showed, that thou mightest know that the

" Lord he is God ; there is none else beside him".—Deut. iv. 35.

" He is God in Heaven above, and upon the earth beneath : " there is none else".—Deut. iv. 39.

" See now that I, even I, am he, and there is no God with me". Deut. xxxii. 39.

" For who in the Heaven can be compared unto Jehovah".— Psalm lxxxix. 6.

" For Jehovah, your God, is God of gods and Lord of lords". —Deut. x. 17.

" Wherefore thou art great, O Lord God : for there is none " like thee, neither is there any God beside thee".—2 Sam. vii. 22.

" To whom then will ye liken God ? or what likeness will ye " compare unto him" ?—Isa. xl. 18.

" To whom will ye liken me, and make me equal, and compare " me, that we may be like".—Isa. xlvi. 5.

" I am God and there is none else : I am God, and there is " none like me".—Isa. xlvi. 9.

" There is none like unto thee, O Jehovah.........there is none " like unto thee".—Jer. x. 6, 7.

" My Father", said Christ, " who gave them me is GREATER " THAN ALL".—John x. 29.

" I go unto the Father : for my FATHER IS GREATER THAN " I".—John xiv. 28.

The preceding passages demonstrate that no one, either in heaven above or on the earth beneath, must be compared to God, as equal with Him. . . . .   The concluding passages of this section of our argument represent God speaking of himself, and being spoken of, in the strictest sense of *oneness*.   The last few passages show that Jesus Christ is not included in the scripture idea of God.

"And God said unto Moses, I am that I am".—Ex. iii. 14.

" *I* am the Almighty God".—Gen. xvii. 1.

" *I* am Jehovah thy God".—Ex. xx. 2.

" See now that *I*, even *I*, am he".—Deut. xxxii. 39.

" Yet *I* am Jehovah thy God, from the land of Egypt, and thou " shalt know no God but me".—Hos. xiii. 4.

" Now will *I* rise, saith Jehovah; now will *I* lift up myself".— Isa. xxxiii. 10.

"*I* form the light, and create darkness; *I* make peace, and " create evil; *I* Jehovah do all these things".—Isa. xlv. 7.

"Am *I* a God at hand, saith Jehovah, and not a God afar " off........Do not *I* fill heaven and earth".—Jer. xxiii. 23, 24.

"Blessed be *thou*, Jehovah God of Israel our father, for ever and " ever. *Thine*, O Jehovah, is the greatness and the power;...... " *thine* is the kingdom, O Jehovah, and *thou* art exalted above " all".—1 Chron. xxix. 10, 11.

" Father, (said Jesus) the hour is come ; glorify *thy* Son, that " *thy* Son also may glorify *thee*, as *thou* hast given him power " over all flesh".—John xvii. 1, 2.

" God hath made that same Jesus, whom ye hath crucified " both Lord and Christ".—Acts ii. 36.

" Ye are Christ's, and Christ is God's".—1 Cor. iii. 23.

" The head of every man is Christ......and the head of Christ " is God".—1 Cor. xi. 3.

" God, even thy God hath anointed *thee* (*i.e.*, Jesus Christ) with " the oil of gladness above thy fellows".—Heb. i. 9.

" The LORD GOD ALMIGHTY, and the *Lamb*, are the temple " of it".—Rev. xxi. 22.

"Now unto the King eternal, immortal, invisible, the ONLY " WISE GOD, be honour and glory for ever and ever".—1 Tim. i. 17.

THE HOLY SPIRIT.

As God, our Heavenly Father, is THE INFINITE SPIRIT who fills all space and time, we are inclined to think it must be an exceedingly difficult task to find in the Bible proofs of another Infinite Spirit, "the third person in the Trinity". It may have been some such thought as this which led Jeremy Taylor (" Works ", xiii. 143) to say, "That the Holy Ghost is God, is nowhere " said in Scripture. That the Holy Ghost is to be invocated, is " nowhere commanded ; nor any example of its being done " recorded ". There is nothing more evident, in the writings of what are called the ante-Nicene fathers, than the fact that Irenæus, Origen, Tertullian, Athenagoras, &c. &c., never thought of the Holy Ghost as equal to the Father. In the New Testament the Holy Spirit is spoken of as sent by the Father, as the gift of the Father—that is, subordinate to the Father. So, too, the Son is repeatedly spoken of as subordinate to the Father, and as deriving all his power and authority from the Father. Trinitarians say, indeed, that these texts refer only to the Son's human nature, and not to his supposed Divine one. But, in the case of the Holy Spirit, no such evasion can be resorted to. Moreover, if the Three Persons of the Trinity be co-equal, is it not very strange that there should be passages so strong, and so numerous, in assertion of the inferiority and sub-jection of the Son and Spirit to the Father, and yet that there is not one passage in the whole Bible that speaks of any inferiority or subjection, real or apparent, of the Father to the Son or the Spirit? We are bound again to repeat that all the weight of Bible evidence is against the hypothesis of a second infinite spirit, equal to "the God and Father of all flesh".

The doctrine of a Triune Deity which affirms the Holy Spirit to be a *third person* in the Godhead, is altogether one of infer-ence; and it involves the mind in the most complete confu-sion, making more than one, eternal omnipotent, omnipresent God. "God is a Spirit", the Holy Spirit, and it is unscriptural to say that there is more than One Infinite Spirit. In the following passages the words "Spirit" and "Holy Ghost" are used for God himself.

"For what man knoweth the things of a man, save the spirit of "man which is in him" (*i.e.* except the man himself), "even so "the things of God knoweth no man, but the Spirit of God", (*i.e.* but God himself.)—1 Cor. ii. 11.

"Why hath Satan filled thy heart to lie to the Holy Ghost?...... "Thou hast not lied unto man but unto God".—Acts v. 3, 4.

"Know ye not that ye are the temple of God, and that the "Spirit of God dwelleth in you".—1 Cor. iii. 16.

"By his Spirit he hath garnished the heavens", (*i.e. God made the heavens.*)—Job xxvi. 13.

"The Spirit of God hath made me", (*i.e. God me.*)—Job xxxiii. 4.

Christ said, "I cast out devils by the spirit of God".—Matt. xii. 28. These were miracles, we learn, *which God did by him.*

"Whither shall I go from thy *Spirit*, or whither shall I flee "from thy *presence*", (*i.e.* from thyself.)—Ps. cxxxix. 7.

" My Spirit shall not always strive with man", (*i.e.* I will not always strive with man.)—Gen. vi. 3.

" Holy men of God spake as they were moved by the Holy " Ghost ", (*i.e.* by God.)—2 Pet. i. 21.

In reading the Scriptures we find that all these works ascribed to the *Spirit* are also said to be done by the *Power, Understanding, Word, Hand, Finger* and *Breath* of God ; can any person seriously believe these to be distinct personalities in the Godhead? Do they not simply mean God himself?

We also perceive that in the Bible, " *the Spirit of God*" frequently signifies *holy influence, strength, comfort, truth, miraculous power, &c., &c.,* which God is said to *send, give, pour out, shed forth, baptize with,* and *anoint with.* The following passages clearly sustain this view :—

" Thou gavest also thy *Good Spirit* to instruct them ".— Neh. ix. 20.

" I will *pour* out *My Spirit* upon all flesh ; and your sons and " your daughters shall prophesy, your old men shall dream " dreams, your young men shall see visions ".—Joel ii. 28.

" And the spirit of the Lord shall rest upon him, the *Spirit* " *of wisdom* and understanding, the *Spirit of knowledge* and the " fear of the Lord ".—Isa. xi. 2.

" Would God that all Jehovah's people were prophets, and " that Jehovah would *put his Spirit* upon them ", (*i.e.* give them wisdom of speech.)—Numb. xi. 29.

" And the Spirit of the Lord came mightily upon him (Sam- " son) and he rent the lion as he would a kid ", (*i.e.* God gave him strength.)—Judges xiv. 6.

" The Spirit of the Lord came upon Gideon, and he blew a " trumpet ; and Abiezer was gathered after him".—Judges vi. 34.

" The *Spirit of the Lord* is upon me, because he hath *anointed* " me to preach the gospel to the poor ; and hath sent me to heal " the broken hearted, to preach deliverance to the captives, and " the recovering of sight to the blind, to set at liberty them that " are bruised ".—Luke iv. 18.

" He whom God hath sent speaketh the words of God ; for " God *giveth* not the *Spirit* by measure unto him ".—Jn. iii. 34.

" God *anointed* Jesus of Nazareth with the *Holy Spirit* and " with *Power*".—Acts x. 38.

" If ye then, being evil, know how to give good gifts unto your
" children, how much more shall your heavenly Father *give the*
" *Holy Spirit* to them that ask him ".—Luke xi. 13.

" Now we have received, not the Spirit of the world, but the
" Spirit which is of God ; that we might know the things that
" are freely given to us of God ".—1 Cor. ii. 12.

" I will pray the Father, and he shall *give* you another *Com-*
"*forter*, that he may abide with you for ever, even the *Spirit*
" *of Truth* ".—John xiv. 16 , 17.

" When the Comforter is come, whom I will send unto you
" from the Father, even the *Spirit of Truth* which *proceedeth*
" from the Father ".—John xv. 26.

" Howbeit, when he, the *Spirit of Truth, is come,* he will
" guide you into all truth ".—John xvi. 13.

No one need wonder that the influence of the Holy Spirit is
spoken of occasionally as a person, when they know that *Sin,*
Death, Wisdom, and *Charity*, though inanimate things and quali-
ties, are often so spoken of.

THE DEITY OF JESUS CHRIST.

THE only source of authority that can be trusted on so grave
a question as that of the Deity of Christ, is the New Testament.
We fail to discover any evidence of Christ's being Almighty
God, but we do find very much to the contrary, in the Sacred
Volume. We are not alone in this position. The point we have
in view is simply this—that many eminent Trinitarians distinctly
admit that our Lord *never* taught his disciples, during his
ministry, that he was God. And then, again, we have another
class of authorities, equally orthodox, who show that the epistles
do not promulgate any new doctrine about the person of Christ,
not found in the Gospels. If our religion has to bear the stamp
of " *Evangelical* ", we must let it rest on the statements of
Christ as recorded by the Evangelists. We may cite again :—

Dr. Bennet (" Discourse of the Trinity ", ch. viii. p. 94), who says :
" During the time of our Saviour's ministry, the disciples did
" not believe he was anything more than a mere man, conducted
" and assisted by the Spirit of God "; and " There is not in all

G

"the New Testament one passage which implies that the
"disciples during his ministry believed him to have had any
"divine nature".

Bishop Burgess ("Plain Argument for the Divinity of Christ",
§ 6), admits, "The apostles appear not to have known that Christ
"was God till after his resurrection and ascension".

The late Archbishop of Canterbury, Dr. Longley, makes the
following admission in "The Brothers' Controversy" :—"The
"little impression which our Saviour's miracles made upon the
"apostles, and the wavering and unsettled conviction of their
"minds as to his being the Messiah after all, is evident from many
"passages". . . . "The objection you have made against
"the doctrine of Christ's divine nature, from its not being dwelt
"upon in the Acts of the Apostles, has often presented itself to
"me". It would be no difficult task to add further testimony, from
Trinitarians themselves, that in the first five books of the New
Testament, there is a deficiency of evidence of Christ being God.

The late Bishop Hampden wrote ("Bampton Lecture",
pp. 374-5) : "No one perhaps will maintain that there is any
"new truth of Christianity set forth in the Epistles ; any truth,
"I mean, which does not pre-suppose the whole truth of
"human salvation by Jesus Christ as already determined and
"complete". G. Townsend bears similar testimony in saying,
("New Testament Arranged", vol. ii. 24), "We must not regard
"the Epistles as communications of religious doctrine not
"disclosed before, as displaying the perfection of a system of
"which merely the rude elements had been inducted in the
"writings of the four Evangelists".

We are persuaded that there is no proposition capable of such
abundant and clear proof from the New Testament as this, that
Christ is not God. We know the question may be proposed to
us, "If Christ is not a Deity, what is He?" Great divergence of
opinion prevails on this subject ; but it is not necessary to settle
it at present, whilst we are dealing with what is really the fundamental practical doctrine, viz., that the Father alone is the
Supreme Deity and the sole object of Christian worship.

PROOFS THAT CHRIST WAS NOT GOD.

Because Christ most clearly showed he was not God.—The

Jews who were seeking a charge against him said, "he made himself God"; Christ immediately refuted the falsehood,—" Jesus
"answered them is it not written in your law, I said, Ye are gods;
"if he called them gods unto whom the word of God came, and
"the scripture cannot be broken; say ye of him, whom the Father
"hath sanctified and sent into the world, Thou blasphemest;
"because I said, I am the Son of God".—Jn. x. 34, 36. He whom
Christ addressed in prayer, he addressed as "THE ONLY TRUE
"God".—Jn. xvii. 3. "He came from God, and went to God".
—Jn. xiii. 3. "I came out from God".—Jn. xvi. 27. "And
"Jesus said unto him, Why callest thou me good? there is none
"good but one, that is, God".—Mark x. 18. "And about the
"ninth hour Jesus cried with a loud voice, saying, Eli, Eli, lama,
"sabachthani? that is to say, My God, my God, why hast thou
"forsaken me"?—Matt. xxvii. 46. "Jesus saith unto her, Touch
"me not; for I am not yet ascended unto my Father: but go to
"my brethren, and say unto them, I ascend unto my Father and
"your Father; and to my God and your God".—Jn. xx. 17.

Because the New Testament in numerous passages declares that
God is the God and Father of Jesus Christ.—"The God and
"Father of our Lord Jesus Christ, which is blessed for evermore,
"knoweth that I lie not".—2 Cor. xi. 31. "Blessed be the God
"and Father of our Lord Jesus Christ, who hath blest us with
"all spiritual blessings in heavenly places in Christ".—Eph. i. 3.
"That the God of our Lord Jesus Christ, the Father of glory,
"may give unto you the spirit of wisdom".—Eph. i. 17. "That
"ye may with one mind, and one mouth, glorify God, even the
"Father of our Lord Jesus Christ".—Rom. xv. 6. "Blessed be
"the God and Father of our Lord Jesus Christ, which according
"to his abundant mercy hath begotten us again unto a lively
"hope by the resurrection of Jesus Christ from the dead".—
1 Pet. i. 3.

Because the Scriptures teach us there is but ONE GOD, *and in*
the same sentence affirm that Christ is not that God.—"To us
"there is but one God, the Father of whom are all things, and we
"in him; and one Lord Jesus Christ".—1 Cor. viii. 6. "For
"there is one God and one mediator between God and men, the
"man Christ Jesus".—1 Tim. 2, 5. "One Lord, one Faith, one
"Baptism, one God and Father of all".—Eph. iv. 5, 6.

Because the Scriptures testify that Jesus grew and increased in favour with God. How could he then be God?—"And Jesus "increased in wisdom and stature, and in favour with God and "man".—Luke ii. 52. "And the child (Jesus) grew and waxed "strong in spirit, filled with wisdom : and the grace of God was "upon him".—Luke ii. 40.

Because the high names, and offices, and greatness of Christ, are said to be given to him by God.—"Wherefore God also hath "highly exalted him, and given him a name which is above every "name".—Philippians ii. 9. "For it pleased the Father that in "him should all fulness dwell".—Col. i. 19. "Therefore let all "the house of Israel know assuredly, that God hath made that "same Jesus, whom ye hath crucified, both Lord and Christ".—Acts ii. 36. "The God of Abraham, and of Isaac, and of Jacob ; "the God of our fathers hath glorified his Son Jesus".—Acts iii. 13. "Him hath God exalted with his right hand to be "a Prince and a Saviour".—Acts v. 31.

Because the New Testament teaches that all power and authority possessed by Christ were given to him by God.—"Then answered "Jesus and said unto them, Verily, verily, I say unto you, the "Son can do nothing of himself, but what he seeth the Father "do".—Jn. v. 19. "I can of mine own self do nothing".—Jn. v. 30. "And (God) hath put all things under his feet, and "gave him to be the head over all things to the Church".—Eph. i. 22. "For though he was crucified through weakness, "yet he liveth by the power of God".—2 Cor. xiii. 4. "I have "power to lay it (his life) down, and I have power to take it "again. This commandment have I received of my Father".—John x. 18.

Because Jesus Christ says he is inferior and subordinate to the Father.—"My Father is greater than I".—Jn. xiv. 28. "To sit "on my right hand and on my left, is not mine to give, but it "shall be given to them, for whom it is prepared of my Father". Matt. xx. 23. "But of that day and that hour (of judgment) "knoweth no man, no, not the angels which are in heaven, "neither the Son, but the Father".—Mark xiii. 32. "My Father "is greater than all".—Jn. x. 29.

Because Christ worshipped and prayed to God.—"Jesus went "out into a mountain to pray, and continued all night in prayer

"to God".—Luke vi. 12. "At that time Jesus answered and
"said, I thank thee, O Father, Lord of heaven and earth".—
Matt. xi. 25. "Jesus prayed, saying, Father, if thou be willing,
"remove this cup from me : nevertheless not my will, but thine
"be done".—Luke xxii. 42. "Christ in the days of his flesh,
"when he had offered up prayers and supplications, with strong
"crying and tears, unto HIM that was able to save".—
Heb. v. 7.

Because Christ has taught us not to pray to him, but to God.—
"In that day ye shall ask me nothing. Verily, verily, I say unto
"you, Whatsoever ye shall ask the Father, in my name, he will
"give it you".—Jn. xvi. 23. "The hour cometh, and now is,
"when the true worshippers shall worship the Father in spirit
"and in truth".—Jn. iv. 23. "As he was praying in a certain
"place, when he ceased, one of his disciples said unto him, Lord
"teach us to pray, as John also taught his disciples. And he
"said unto them, When ye pray, say, *our Father* which art in
"Heaven".—Luke xi. 1, 2. "For this cause I bow my knees
"unto the Father of our Lord Jesus Christ".—Eph. iii. 14.

Because the very name CHRIST *shows he is not God, but
anointed of God.—*"Thou (Christ) hast loved righteousness,
"and hated iniquity ; therefore God, even thy God, hath anointed
"thee with the oil of gladness above thy fellows".—Heb. i. 9.
"How God anointed Jesus of Nazareth with the Holy Ghost
"and with power : who went about doing good . . . for
"God was with him".—Acts x. 38. "For of a truth against thy
"holy child Jesus, whom thou hast anointed".—Acts iv. 27.

*Because Jesus Christ is represented by himself as distinct from
God as one witness in a court is from another.—*"It is also written
"in your law that the testimony of two men is true. I am one
"who bears witness of myself, and the Father that sent me
"beareth witness of me".—Jn. viii. 17, 18.

*Because in numerous passages of Scripture Christ is repre-
sented as appointed Judge of all by God.—*"For the Father
"judgeth no man, but hath committed all judgment to the Son".
—Jn. v. 22. "And he commanded us to preach unto the people,
"and to testify that it is he which was ordained of God to be the
"Judge of quick and dead".—Acts x. 42. "Because he hath
"appointed a day in which he will judge the world in righteous-

"ness, by that man whom he hath ordained ; whereof he hath
"given assurance unto all men, in that he hath raised Him from
"the dead".—Acts xvii. 31.

Because the name SON OF GOD *shows he is not God.*—"But
"whom say ye that I am? And Simon Peter answered and
"said, Thou art the Christ, the Son of the living God".—
Matt. xvi. 15, 16. "For he received from God the Father honour
"and glory when there came such a voice to him from the excel-
"lent glory, This is my beloved Son, in whom I am well
"pleased".—2 Peter i. 17. "Of a truth thou art the Son of
God".—Matt. xiv. 33.

*Because Christ was taught of God the doctrines he taught to
Men.*—"I do nothing of myself ; but as my Father hath taught
"me, I speak these things".—Jn. viii. 28. "Jesus answered
"them, and said, My doctrine is not mine, but his that sent me".
Jn. vii. 16. "For I have not spoken of myself ; but the Father
"which sent me, he gave me a commandment, what I should
"say, and what I should speak".—Jn. xii. 49.

*Because numerous passages show a clear distinction between
God and Christ.*—"Grace be unto you, and peace from God our
"Father, and from the Lord Jesus Christ".—1 Cor. i. 3. "To
"all that be in Rome, beloved of God, called to be saints :
"Grace to you and peace from God our Father, and the Lord
"Jesus Christ".—Rom. i. 7. "Unto Timothy, my own son in the
"faith: Grace, mercy, and peace from God our Father and Jesus
"Christ our Lord".—1 Tim. i. 2. "Paul, and Silvanus, and
"Timotheus, unto the Church of the Thessalonians which is in
"God the Father and the Lord Jesus Christ".—1 Thess. i. 1.

Because Christ always declared he was only the sent of God.—
"For he whom God hath sent speaketh the words of God : for
"God giveth not the spirit by measure unto him".—Jn. iii. 34.
"And he that sent me is with me".—Jn. viii. 29. "Then said
"Jesus to them again, Peace be unto you : As my Father hath
"sent me, even so send I you".—Jn. xx. 21. "I am not come
"of myself but he that sent me is true".—Jn. vii. 28. "This is
"the work of God, that ye believe on him whom he hath sent".
—Jn. vi. 29.

Because the Apostles always speak of Christ as less than God.
—"But I would have you know that the head of every man is

"Christ ; and the head of the woman is the man ; and the head
"of Christ is God ".—1 Cor. xi. 3. "And ye are Christ's, and
"Christ is God's ".—1 Cor. iii. 23. "For he (God) hath put all
"things under his (Christ's) feet. But when he saith all things
"are put under him, it is manifest that he is excepted, which did
"put all things under him ".—1 Cor. xv. 27.

*Because Christ is called the Image of God ; and an image can-
not be that of which it is the likeness.*—"Who (Christ) is the
image of the invisible God ".—Col. i. 15. "Lest the light of the
"glorious gospel of Christ, who is the image of God, should
"shine unto them ".—2 Cor. iv. 4. "Who (Christ) being the
" brightness of his glory, and the express image of his person ".
—Heb. i. 3.

*Because the uniform teaching of the Scripture is that God
raised Jesus Christ from the dead.*—"This Jesus hath God raised
" up, whereof we all are witnesses ".—Acts ii. 32. "And (ye)
" killed the Prince of Life, whom God hath raised from the dead ".
—Acts iii. 15. "Unto you first God having raised up his Son
" Jesus, sent him to bless you, in turning away every one of you
" from his iniquities ".—Acts iii. 26. "The God of our fathers
" raised up Jesus whom ye slew and hanged on a tree ".—
Acts v. 30. "And God hath both raised up the Lord, and will
" also raise up us by his own power ".—1 Cor. vi. 14.

*Because the Apostles often speak of Christ as a Man, and in
the same sentence show he is not God.*—"Jesus of Nazareth, a
" man approved of God among you by miracles and wonders and
" signs, which God did by him ".—Acts ii. 22. "But this man
" after he had offered one sacrifice for sins for ever, sat down on
" the right hand of God ".—Heb. x. 12.

*Because Jesus Christ never taught he was God, but most dis-
tinctly taught he was a Man, and the Son of Man.*—"But now
" ye seek to kill me, a man that hath told you the truth, which I
" have heard of God ".—Jn. viii. 40. "Therefore the Son of
" Man is Lord also of the Sabbath ".—Mark ii. 28.

Because Christ was a Prophet as Moses was a Prophet.—
" The Lord thy God will raise up unto thee a prophet from the
" midst of thee, of thy brethren like unto me. . . . I will
" raise them up a prophet from among their brethren, like unto
" thee, and will put my words into his mouth ".—Deut. xviii. 15, 18.

Stephen testifies that Christ is that prophet. "This is that "Moses which said unto the children of Israel, A prophet shall "the Lord your God raise unto you of your brethren, like unto "me".—Acts vii. 37.

Because the Sacred Scriptures represent Christ as coming not to do his own will, but the will of God.—"Jesus saith unto them, "My meat is to do the will of him that sent me".—Jn. iv. 34. "For I came down from heaven not to do mine own will, but the "will of him that sent me".—Jn. vi. 38. "I seek not mine own "will but the will of the Father which hath sent me".—Jn. v. 30. "Lo, I come to do thy will, O God".—Heb. x. 7.

Because the Scriptures uniformly represent Christ as being at the right hand of God. How then can he be God ?—"So then "after the Lord had spoken unto them, he was received up into "heaven, and sat on the right hand of God".—Mark xvi. 19. "Hereafter shall the Son of Man sit on the right hand of the "power of God".—Luke xxii. 69. "Therefore being by the "right hand of God".—Acts. ii. 33.

Because the reign of Christ shall come to an end.—"Then "cometh the *end* when he shall have delivered up the kingdom "to God, even the Father; when he shall have put down all rule "and all authority and power".—"And when all things shall be "subdued unto him, then shall the Son also himself be subject "unto him that put all things under him, that God may be all in "all".—1 Cor. xv. 24, 28.

Because the whole of the passages adduced for the deity of Christ are capable of an easy explanation, so that every text supposed to support the doctrine of the Godhead of Christ has been explained by Trinitarian theologians in a different sense from that which supports this doctrine. And because we find it conceded in the commentaries of Trinitarians that *our* proof texts cause them insuperable difficulties, so that they retire from their own explanations, expressing dissatisfaction at them and conceding that these texts are not capable of an easy explanation on their hypothesis ; while *their* proof texts are explained away by expositors of their own school.

Because Christ is represented as a Priest. The office of a priest is to minister to God.—Because he is represented as an Apostle appointed of God.—Because he is represented as an

Intercessor with God.—Because he is represented as not the *primary*, but *intermediate*, cause of the benefits he bestows.—Because he denies that he is possessed of independent existence, omnipotence, omnipresence, and omniscience. — Because it is expressly stated, "The Revelation of Jesus Christ *God* "*gave to him*".—Because he is represented as the servant of God.—Because he is represented as receiving honour from God in consequence of doing what pleased God.—Because Christ is represented as having learned obedience by the things which he suffered.—Because St. Paul affirms that Christ now lives unto God and by the power of God. — Because when charged by the Jews with making himself equal with God, he replied, "The Son can do nothing of himself".—Because if the salvation of man depends on believing Christ is God, it is curious that Christ never taught those who surrounded him that he was God ; but when they professed to understand he was making himself God, or equal with God, he immediately denied these charges, so that they might not regard him in that light.—Because no man hath seen God at any time. This cannot be affirmed of Jesus Christ.—Because had the disciples believed him to be Almighty God, they could not have been so *familiar* with him, *argued* with him, *betrayed* him or *denied* him, and *fled* from him, and at first *disbelieved* in his resurrection from the dead. If this is an essential doctrine of Christianity, we cannot understand how the disciples knew nothing of it.—Because we never find the Jews charging the *first Apostles* with teaching that Christ is God, which every Jew *now* charges on the head of Christian teachers.

PRAYER TO CHRIST.

WE have already remarked on the example and command of Christ about prayer to God; and quoted Archbishop Wake, who says (in his work on the Catechism, p. 130), that the Lord's Prayer teaches us "that we should pray " to God only, and to Him as our Father, through Jesus " Christ our Lord". Some years ago (1867), Bishop Colenso was criticised in a correspondence in the *Times* for denying the Scriptural authority of prayer to Christ. In a letter to his critics he challenged them "to produce *one* single instance " in which we are instructed, enjoined, exhorted, or counselled " by our Lord, or by any of his apostles, to pray to the Son or to " the Spirit as we are taught in the passages (to which he had " referred in his former letters) to pray to the Father". Dr. Heurtley, the Oxford Margaret Professor of Divinity, in reply to Bishop Colenso, made the following remarkable admission :— " Now, I frankly concede to him that I have no such instance to produce". See *Times*, of January 25th and January 30th, 1867 We have already shown that other distinguished clergymen say much the same as Bishop Colenso—that there is no precept or command in the Bible that prayer should be offered to any other being than the Father of our Lord Jesus Christ.

The Scriptures are as accessible to all of us as to these learned men. What saith the Scripture?

JESUS CHRIST TAUGHT THAT PRAYER SHOULD BE OFFERED TO THE FATHER ONLY.

" When thou prayest, enter into thy closet, and when thou " hast shut the door, PRAY TO THY FATHER", &c.—Matt. vi. 6.

" After this manner therefore pray ye : OUR FATHER which " art in heaven".—Matt. vi. 9.

" If ye then, being evil, know how to give good gifts unto your " children, how much more shall *your Father* who is in heaven " give good things to them that ask him".—Matt. vii. 11.

" Again I say unto you, that if two of you shall agree on " earth as touching anything that they shall *ask*, it shall be done " for them of *my Father* who is in heaven".—Matt. xviii. 19.

" When ye stand *praying*, forgive if ye have aught against " any, that *your Father* also who is in heaven may forgive you " your trespasses".—Mark xi. 25.

" As he was praying in a certain place, when he ceased, one " of his disciples said unto him, *Lord teach us to pray*, as John " also taught his disciples. And he said unto them, *When you* " *pray, say, Our Father* which art in heaven".—Luke xi. 1, 2.

" The hour cometh, and now is, when the true worshippers

" *shall worship the Father* in spirit and in truth ; for the Father
" seeketh such to worship him".—John iv. 23.

" In that day YE SHALL ASK ME NOTHING. Verily, verily, I
" say unto you, Whatsoever ye shall *ask the Father* in my name,
" he will give it you".—John xvi. 23.

The foregoing passages teach us to pray to the Father and *not*
to pray to the Son. The following are of the same nature
enjoining prayer to the Father in the *name* of the Son or through
Jesus Christ.

" Whatsoever ye shall *ask of the Father* in my name he may
" give it you".—John xv. 16.

" At that day ye shall ask in my name : and I say not unto
" you, that I will pray the Father for you, for the Father him-
" self loveth you".—John xvi. 26, 27.

" And whatsoever ye shall ask in my name, that will I do, that
" the Father may be glorified in the Son".—John xiv. 13.

" Giving thanks always for all things unto God and the Father
" in the name of our Lord Jesus Christ".—Eph. v. 20.

" And whatsoever ye do in word or deed, do all in the name
" of the Lord Jesus, giving thanks to God and the Father by
" him".—Col. iii. 17.

" I *thank* God, through Jesus Christ our Lord".—Rom. vii. 25.

That one God the Father, the God and Father of our Lord
and Saviour Jesus Christ, is *alone* entitled to supreme worship,
we learn from the Old and New Testament. The example of
Christ, and his disciples, and apostles, in addressing their praise
and prayer to God, ought to suffice on this question. The
following passages will show the

EXAMPLE OF CHRIST.

" At that time Jesus answered and said, I thank thee, O
" *Father, Lord of heaven and earth,* because thou hast hid these
" things from the wise and prudent, and hast revealed them unto
" babes".—Matt. xi. 25.

" And it came to pass in those days, that he (Jesus) went out
" into a mountain to pray, and continued all night in prayer to
" God".—Luke vi. 12.

" And he went a little farther, and fell on his face, and prayed,

" saying, *O my Father*, if it be possible, let this cup pass from
" me ; nevertheless not as I will, but as thou wilt ".—Matt.
xxvi. 39.

" Thinkest thou that I cannot now pray to my Father, and he
" shall presently give me more than twelve legions of angels ".—
Matt. xxvi. 53.

" He prayed, saying, Father, if thou be willing, remove this
" cup from me : nevertheless not my will, but thine, be done ".—
Luke xxii. 42.

" These words spake Jesus, and lifted up his eyes to heaven,
" and said, Father the hour is come ; glorify thy Son, that thy
" Son also may glorify thee ".—John xvii. 1.

" Now is my soul troubled ; and what shall I say ? Father,
" save me from this hour ; but for this cause came I unto this
" hour ".—John xii. 27.

" And Jesus lifted up *his* eyes, and said, Father, I thank thee
" that thou hast heard me. And I knew that thou hearest me
" always : and because of the people which stand by I said it,
" that they may believe that thou hast sent me ".—John xi. 41, 42.

" And I will *pray the Father*, and he will give you another
" comforter ".—John xiv. 16.

" And about the ninth hour, Jesus cried with a loud voice,
" saying,......My God ! my God ! why hast thou forsaken me " ?
—Matt. xxvii. 46.

" Then said Jesus, *Father*, forgive them ; for they know not
" what they do ".—Luke xxiii. 34.

" And when Jesus had cried with a loud voice, he said, Father,
" into thy hands I commend my spirit ; and having said thus,
" he gave up the ghost ".—Luke xxiii. 46.

EXAMPLE OF APOSTLES AND DISCIPLES OF CHRIST.

" They (apostles) lifted up their voice to God with one accord,
" and said, Lord thou art God who hast made heaven, and earth,
" and the sea ;.........grant that signs and wonders may be done
" by the name of thy holy child, Jesus ".—Acts iv. 24, 30.

" But this I (Paul) confess unto thee, that after the way which
" they call heresy, *so worship I the God of my fathers*, believing
" all things which are written in the law and the prophets ".—
Acts xxiv. 14.

"I *thank my God,* through Jesus Christ for you all, that your
"faith is spoken of throughout the whole world".—Rom. i. 8.

"Now the God of patience and consolation grant you to be
"like minded one toward another, according to Christ Jesus ;
"that ye may with one mind and one mouth *glorify God, even*
"*the Father of our Lord Jesus Christ*".—Rom. xv. 5, 6.

"*To God only wise,* be glory, through Jesus Christ for ever".
—Rom. xvi. 27

"*Blessed be God, even the Father of our Lord Jesus Christ.*
"The Father of mercies and the God of all comfort".—2 Cor. i. 3.

"That the *God of our Lord Jesus Christ, the Father of*
"*glory*, may give unto you the spirit of wisdom, and revelation
"in the knowledge of him".—Eph. i. 17.

"Now unto HIM that is able to do exceeding abundantly
"above all that we ask or think, according to the power that
"worketh in us, *unto Him be glory in the Church* by Christ
"Jesus, throughout all ages world without end".—Eph. iii. 20, 21.

"Now unto the King eternal, immortal, invisible, the only
"wise God, *be honour and glory for ever and ever*".—1 Tim. i. 17.

"For this cause *I bow my knees unto the Father of our Lord*
"*Jesus Christ*, of whom the whole family in heaven and earth is
"named, that he would grant you, according to the riches of his
"glory, to be strengthened with might by his spirit in the inner
"man".—Eph. iii. 14, 16.

ESSENCE OF RELIGION.

IN most treatises on religion we meet with summaries of what
may be called "the essence of religion"; and with statements
which place the essentials of belief and duty on a basis as available to those who reject the doctrine of the Trinity as to those
who accept it.

"Of what is essential to salvation, it is not difficult to judge.
"The quiet of the conscience requires, that the information on
"this subject should be clear and precise : whatever is beyond
"is involved in comparative obscurity, and subject to doubtful
"disputation".—*Robert Hall.*

"1. We think nothing necessary to be known or believed for

" salvation but what God hath revealed. 2. We therefore em-
" brace all those who in sincerity receive the word of truth
" revealed in the Scripture, and obey the light which enlightens
" every man that comes into the world", &c.—*John Locke.*

" Remember, the essence of religion is a heart void of offence
"towards God and man. Hold fast by this sheet anchor of
" happiness—religion ; you will often want it in the times of
" most danger—the storms and tempests of life. . . . . You
" have been taught, indeed, that right belief, or orthodoxy, will,
" like charity, cover a multitude of sins. Be not deceived. The
"chattering of some unintelligible sounds called creeds, and
" unfeigned assent and consent to whatever the Church enjoins
" —religious worship and consecrated feasts—repenting on a
" death-bed—pardons rightly sued out, and absolutions authori-
" tatively given—have done more towards making and con-
" tinuing men vicious than all the natural passions and infidelity
" put together ".—*Lord Chatham.*

" Religion is the concern of all men ; it ought, therefore, to be
" clear and plain. An obscure religion is of little or no value ;
" indeed, it seems to me one of the greatest absurdities that can
" be conceived. If God make a revelation intended for the
" general benefit of mankind, one would expect it should be
" clear. I have a strong persuasion the gospel was plain at
" first. If Christianity is not plain now, I apprehend it must be
" our own fault. A doctrine that contains plain directions of
" duty and plain promises of reward, sufficient to encourage to
" duty in all circumstances, to strengthen against temptations, to
" give comfort under affliction, to calm the affections, this is true
" religion ".—*Dr. Nath. Lardner.*

" The Christian religion, according to my mind, is a very
" simple thing, intelligible to the meanest capacity, and what, if
" we are at pains to join practice to knowledge, we may make
" ourselves thoroughly acquainted with, without turning over
" many books. I wonder to see so many men, eminent both for
" their piety and for their capacity, labouring to make a mystery
" of this divine institution. If God vouchsafes to reveal himself
" to mankind, can we suppose that he chooses to do so in such

" a manner as that none but the learned and contemplative can
" understand him? The generality of mankind can never, in
" any possible circumstances, have leisure or capacity for learning
" or profound contemplation. If, therefore, we make Christianity
" a mystery, we exclude the greater part of mankind from the
" knowledge of it ; which is directly contrary to the intention of
" its author ".—*Dr. Beattie.*

We have given the above extracts because it is, at times,
assumed that the rejection of the doctrine of the Trinity is in-
compatible with religious faith. That good and pious man John
Wesley seemed to think so, for he says, in his sermon on the
Trinity, "I do not see how it is possible for any one to have
vital religion who denies that these three are one ". But there
are other eminent and religious men who have had a different
opinion and have clearly expressed it.

" England may well be proud of having had Milton, Locke,
"and Newton for the champions of its faith and its Protestantism".
—*Brewster.*

" When I look at the reception, by the Unitarians, both of the
" Old and New Testament, I cannot for my part, strongly as I
" dislike their theology, deny to those who acknowledge the basis
"of divine fact the name of Christian ".—*Bishop Hampden.*

"An Unitarian, as such, is a Christian ; that is, if a man
" follows Christ's law, and believes his words according to his
" conscientious sense of their meaning, he is a Christian ; and
" though I may think he understands Christ's words amiss, yet
" that is a question of interpretation, and no more ".—*Dr.
Arnold.*

" I must also do this right to the Unitarians as to own, that
" their rules in morality are exact and severe ; that they are
" generally men of probity, justice, and charity, and seem to be
" very much in earnest in pressing the obligations to very high
" degrees in virtue.—*Bishop Burnet.*

" I shall ever think and ever speak of Mr. Wakefield (the
" Unitarian) as a very profound scholar, as a most honest man,
" and as a Christian who united knowledge with zeal, piety with

" benevolence, and the deep simplicity of a child with the
" fortitude of a martyr ".—*Dr. Samuel Parr.*

" With regard to their moral code, the principles of the
" Unitarians do not seem to admit their loosening, in the least,
" the bonds of duty : on the contrary, they appear to be actuated
" by an earnest desire to promote practical religion. Love is,
" with them, the fulfilling of the law ; and the habitual practice
" of virtue, from a principle of love to God and benevolence to
" man, is, in their judgment, the sum and substance of Chris-
" tianity ".—*Dr. Adams.*

" When misguided men, of more zeal than knowledge, would
" thus distinguish the Unitarian from the Christian, whom, I will
" ask, do we fondly cite as our highest authorities, when we are
" engaged in defending our religion against its infidel adver-
" saries ? In arguing with these upon the evidences, how often
" have we said, what better would you have than that which
" satisfied the greatest masters of science, the great luminaries
" of law ? Who was ever a better judge of legal evidence than
" Hale ; of moral evidence than Locke ; of mathematical and
" physical evidence than Newton ?"—*Lord Brougham.*

" I never attempted to encourage or discourage his (the Duke
" of Grafton's) profession of Unitarian principles : for I was
" happy to see a person of his rank professing, with intelligence
" and with sincerity, Christian principles. If any one thinks
" that a Unitarian is not a Christian, I plainly say, without
" being myself a Unitarian, that I think otherwise ". . . .
" If different men, in carefully and conscientiously examining
" the Scriptures, should arrive at different conclusions, even on
" points of the last importance, we trust that God, who alone
" knows what every man is capab'e of, will be merciful to him
" that is in error. We trust that he will pardon the Unitarian if
" he be in an error, because he has fallen into it from the dread
" of becoming an idolator,—of giving that glory to another which
" he conceives to be due to God alone. If the worshipper of
" Jesus Christ be in an error, we trust that God will pardon his
" mistake ".—*Bishop Watson.*

Christmas, 1882.　　　　　　　　　　　　　　R. S.

www.ingramcontent.com/pod-product-compliance
Lightning Source LLC
Chambersburg PA
CBHW032152010726
47493CB00008BA/2672